Best Editorial Cartoons of the Year

DRAPER HILL
Courtesy Detroit News

BEST EDITORIAL CARTOONS OF THE YEAR

1984 EDITION

Edited by
CHARLES BROOKS

Foreword by KARL HUBENTHAL

PELICAN PUBLISHING COMPANY

GRETNA 1984

Special acknowledgment is made to the following for permission to use copyrighted material in this volume:

Editorial cartoons by Richard Allison, © Army Times; Jim Berry, © NEA; Vic Cantone, © Rothco; Paul Conrad, © Los Angeles Times Syndicate; Hugh Haynie, © Los Angeles Times Syndicate; Gary Huck, © Huck Cartoons; Al Liederman, © Rothco; Dick Locher, © Chicago Tribune; Jeff MacNelly, © Chicago Tribune; Jimmy Margulies, © Rothco; Bill Mitchell, © Ripon Forum and © American Politics; John Milt Morris, © The Associated Press; Jim Orton, © Computerworld; Mike Peters, © United Features; Eldon Pletcher, © Rothco; Jerry Robinson, © Cartoonists and Writers Syndicate; Wayne Stayskal, © Chicago Tribune; Kirk R. Tingblad, © College Press Service; Ed Valtman, © Rothco; Dan Wasserman, © Los Angeles Times Syndicate; and Art Wood, © Farm Bureau News.

Library of Congress Serial Catalog Data

Best editorial cartoons. 1972-
    Gretna [La.] Pelican Pub. Co.
    v. 29 cm. annual-
"A pictorial history of the year."

    1. United States- Politics and government—
1969—Caricatures and Cartoons—Periodicals.
E839.5.B45   320.9'7309240207   73-643645
ISSN 0091-2220   MARC-S

Manufactured in the United States of America
Published by Pelican Publishing Company, Inc.
1101 Monroe Street, Gretna, Louisiana 70053
Designed by Barney McKee

Contents

Foreword

The popular conception of the editorial cartoonist pictures him as an irate crusader, dipping his pen in venom and lashing out in all directions at the collective bad guys of this world. He is regarded as a sort of modern Don Quixote, continually tilting at windmills. He is an eccentric prima donna, not entirely reliable, and something of a zany.

I have been a member of our admittedly strange fraternity for over forty years, so I speak with some authority when I say such a character never has existed—no more so than those *Front Page* archetypes, the drunken reporter and the tyrannical city editor. The mere mechanics of the job leaves little time for screwball antics. Four hours of think time and four hours of drawing is the general work pattern. Add to that the hours of reading, researching, and waiting for editors to get off the phone and you have a full workday by anybody's standards.

Yet the illusion still persists (even among editors) that this ability to make a concise, to-the-point statement each day, couched in a clever drawing, is some sort of odd gift that flows from the cartoonist's hand and head as easily as turning on a spigot. The complexities of creative writing are matters editors can understand, because words are their racket. The ordeal of creative drawing—composition, design, perspective, anatomy—the vehicle we use to present this idea we've been polishing for four hours, is beyond their ken. The suspicion still gnaws at them that somehow we just "knock it out." The point I am belaboring here is that every cartoonist I know is a hard-working person. Ours is not the glamorous profession movies and television picture it to be.

The very nature of his work habits tends to make the editorial cartoonist a loner, and consequently something of an introvert. He is one of a kind in the city room, accepted with considerable suspicion by his fellow journalists because of this strange marriage of writing and drawing skills. Oddly, the degree of introversion seems to be in direct reverse ratio to the inhibitions he loses the moment he takes brush in hand. The angriest of cartoonists are often the meekest, most reluctant of men. I do not mean to imply we are all antisocial. There is no stereotype for our craft. The only common denominator is an aversion to ordered discipline that knows no bounds.

FOREWORD

Consider what the cartoonist is asked to provide each day. His must be a unique comment about the world around him. It must encapsulate and refine a complicated news subject to its basic essence. This idea must be presented in an arresting way and at the same time be clear enough for even the laziest of readers to understand. Unlike the columnist, with his generous allotment of space and his easy access to the "on the other hand" and "according to current estimate" dodges for avoiding outright commitment, the cartoonist cannot equivocate. His is a single-shot statement delivered with a sense of humor.

Most newspapers employ an editorial writing staff composed of several individuals. Each is usually an expert in one particular field. One will be versed in international matters while another will cover the Washington and political scene. Yet another will handle the local editorial subjects. However, the cartoonist is expected to know something about everything. He must be prepared to draw cartoons about international problems, what is going on in Congress, what is happening at city hall—to speak knowledgeably about economics, social change, and scientific progress.

Add still another factor. Television and the wider use of photography in newspapers and magazines have made personalities in the news much more familiar to readers. Their faces—and their physical characteristics—appear nightly in living rooms throughout the country. Now, when the cartoon incorporates images of President Reagan, Tip O'Neill, Margaret Thatcher, or Arafat, the caricatures must be right on. Gone are the days when you could get by with a poor likeness and a label.

Along that same line, editorial writers and columnists can expound knowingly about the space shuttle without having the vaguest idea whether the thruster rockets are in a cluster of three or five, or whether the cargo hatch hinges on the left or right. Not so the cartoonist. Draw it wrong and the observant reader lets you know right away. Besides reading news releases and background articles, we devote considerable time to visual research. Ask any cartoonist's wife about the hours he spends clipping "scrap" for his reference file.

In recent years there has been a virtual renaissance in political cartooning. Sweeping across those tired grey pages like a fresh breeze is a new, comic style that makes the oldtimers look dull by comparison. It's more than just a generation gap in technique of drawing. It's a whole new way of thinking, an entirely different lifestyle. These kids are honed on a type of satire that never existed in my formative years.

There is a greater percentage of good cartoonists working in this country today and a lesser percentage of trite cartoons being produced than at any other time in the history of journalism. There are multiple

reasons why the editorial cartoon of today is superior and more effective. First and most importantly, the cartoon is now a feature unto
itself; seldom, if ever, is it tied to an accompanying editorial. It is a
peek behind the news, so to speak, through the eyes of one artist, not
an editorial board. And it is accepted by the readers as the opinion of
its creator, not necessarily reflecting the policy of the publisher any
more so than, say, any of the political columnists on the same page.
There is a new freedom won by this generation of cartoonists and it is
reflected in their work.

Secondly, we certainly have the material to work with these days,
more subject matter than we can fully cope with. Can you imagine an
editorial cartoon of today extolling the joys of summer and strawberry
shortcake, or the virtues of straw hat day? Or a hundred other inane
subjects the oldtimers were forced to resort to? Maybe, in a sense, we
have it easier than they did. As cartoonists, we deal in fantasy and ex-
aggeration—but what else is the news itself? What stretches credulity
more than a man walking on the moon? How can you exaggerate the
federal deficit figure? What bigger absurdity is there than a world de-
liberately choking itself with its own pollution or a bomb that can wipe
out mankind? When you stop to think about it, the facts on page one
today are already cartoons.

But today's editorial cartoon cannot be just an illustrated headline.
That was the failing of our predecessors. Too often they were illustra-
tors rather than commentators, translating news stories into a kind of
pictorial shorthand of shopworn cliches and symbols. Then they com-
pounded the insult to reader intelligence by covering it all with a mess
of labels. The increasingly aware readership of today demands a more
subtle, knowledgeable product. We try now to bring an opinionated
insight, or at least a gut feeling, to the news that the reader can iden-
tify with. That he will react to. Poster-type ideas are no longer accept-
able.

I don't mean to imply that our predecessors were any less visceral,
in their way, than we are. As Bill Mauldin aptly put it, "Indignation,
sorrow, wrath, and even remorse should so disquiet a good cartoonist's
mile-and-a-half of intestines that he will rush through the darkness looking for the bastards."

They did it, we do it, and the cartoonists of the future will too.
The mood of our nation today is skepticism, not credulity. That is
a most salubrious habitat for the political cartoonist. Long may it last!

KARL HUBENTHAL

Award–Winning Cartoons

1983 PULITZER PRIZE

DICK LOCHER
Editorial Cartoonist
Chicago Tribune

Born June 4, 1929, in Dubuque, Iowa; attended Loras College and the University of Iowa; former Air Force pilot and aircraft designer; studied art at the Chicago Academy of Fine Art and the Art Center of Los Angeles; former president of Novamark, a sales-promotion agency; assistant to Chester Gould, creator of the Dick Tracy comic strip, 1957-61; cartoonist for Dick Tracy comic strip, 1983 to present; editorial cartoonist for the *Chicago Tribune,* 1973 to present; winner of three major cartoon awards in 1983—the Pulitzer Prize, the Sigma Delta Chi Award, and the Overseas Press Club Award; syndicated by the *Chicago Tribune.*

1983 OVERSEAS PRESS CLUB AWARD

DICK LOCHER
Editorial Cartoonist
Chicago Tribune

1982 SIGMA DELTA CHI AWARD
(Selected in 1983)

DICK LOCHER
Editorial Cartoonist
Chicago Tribune

1982 NATIONAL NEWSPAPER AWARD/CANADA

(Selected in 1983)

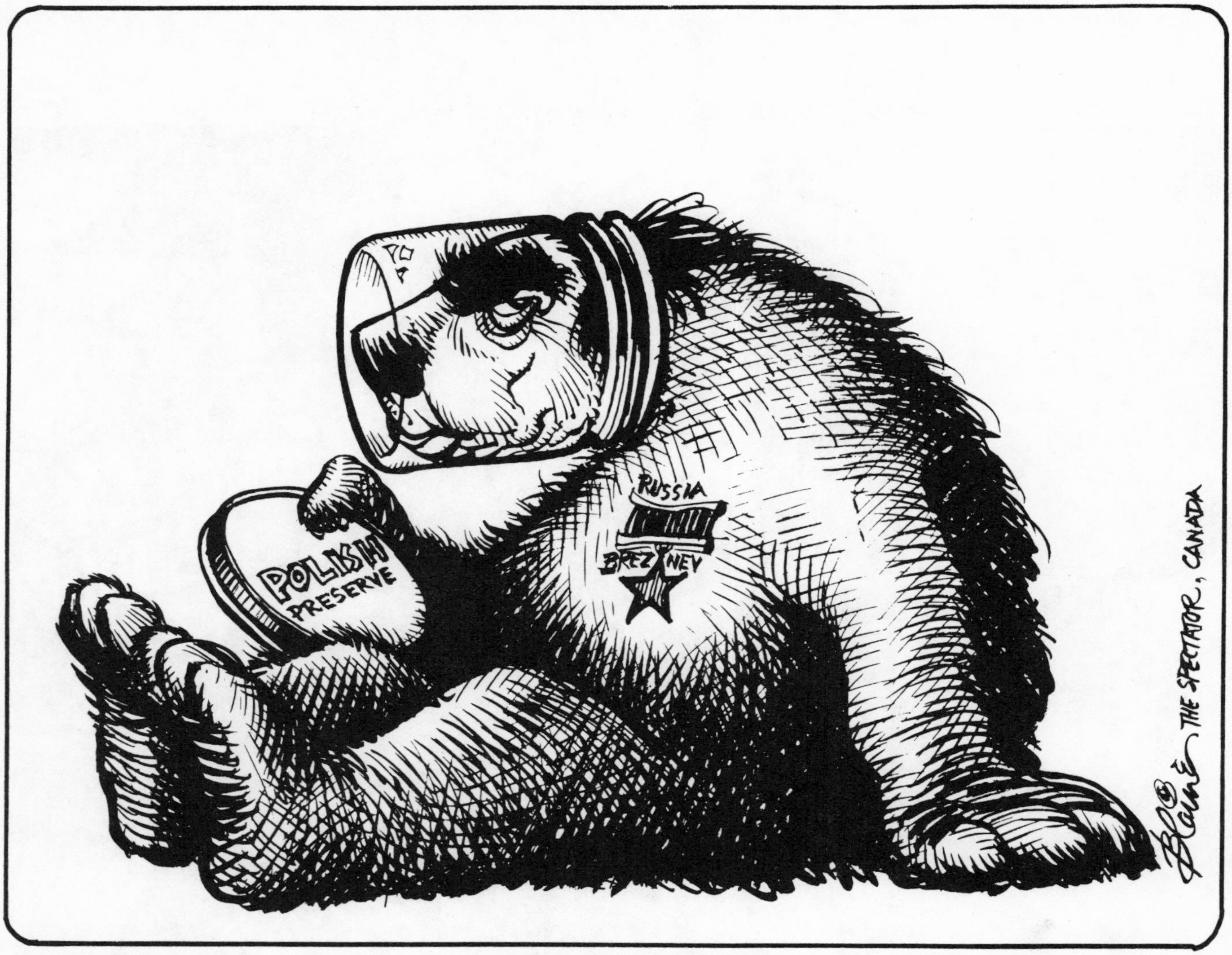
POLISH
PRESERVE
RUSSIA
BREZNEV
THE SPECTATOR, CANADA
BLAINE

BLAINE

Editorial Cartoonist

Hamilton (Ont.) Spectator

Adopted his first name as his full legal identity; winner of National Newspaper Award for cartooning, 1975, 1982; only Canadian cartoonist ever to win the coveted Reuben Award (1970); first ever to win the grand prize in Montreal Salon of Cartoons; black belt instructor in karate; singer, composer, and portrait painter; cartoons syndicated by Miller Services Ltd.

Best Editorial Cartoons of the Year

"TO THE PRESIDENT! WHO IS MAKING EVEN US LOOK GOOD!"

PAUL CONRAD
Courtesy Los Angeles Times

Reagan Administration

During 1983 the Reagan administration was able to slightly reduce the spending growth rate that had been accelerating for years and had shot up dramatically under President Carter. Democrats accused Reagan of hiking defense spending at the expense of social programs. The defense budget did rise by 12.1 percent, but the budgets of six major social programs rose at a higher rate, and others were not far behind. Expenditures for the special supplemental food program for women, infants, and children climbed by nearly 24 percent.

Reagan aides were puzzled by polls indicating that the president was significantly less popular among women than among men. Women's groups, insisting that Reagan was insensitive to women's issues, were told that Reagan had named more women to top political jobs than any previous president, and that his economic programs were doing more for the welfare of women than those promoted by the Democrats.

A major flap arose over the alleged theft of President Carter's briefing papers, which were used by Republicans in the 1980 presidential campaign. David Stockman admitted using the book in playing the role of Carter while preparing Reagan for a series of debates. Reagan denied any knowledge of the matter, and an FBI investigation turned up nothing.

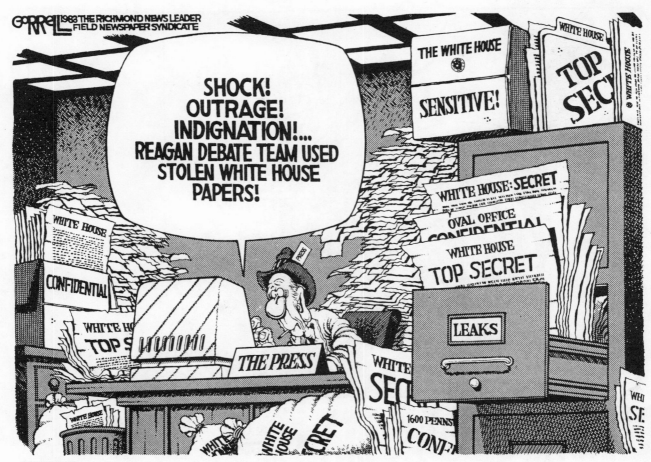

BOB GORRELL
Courtesy Richmond News

BRUCE BEATTIE
Courtesy Daytona Beach News–Journal
©83 Daytona Beach Morning Journal

"I propose we reword the First Amendment and make it: FREEDOM FROM THE PRESS."

JOHN TREVER
Courtesy Albuquerque Journal

DR. STRANGEBUDGET- OR HOW I LEARNED TO STOP WORRYING AND LOVE THE BOMB

GEORGE FISHER
Courtesy Arkansas Gazette

'We'll Get This Country Rolling Again —
Push Harder'

TOM ENGELHARDT
Courtesy St. Louis Post–Dispatch

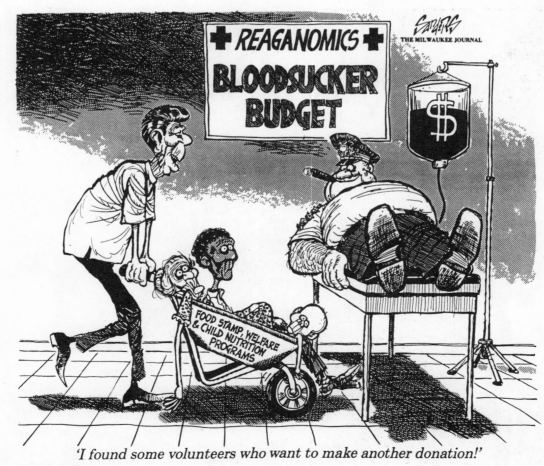

'I found some volunteers who want to make another donation!'

BILL SANDERS
Courtesy Milwaukee Journal

DAN WASSERMAN
© Los Angeles Times Syndicate

JIM BORGMAN
Courtesy Cincinnati Enquirer

DOUG MACGREGOR
Courtesy Norwich Bulletin

'I AM NOT SHOUTING'

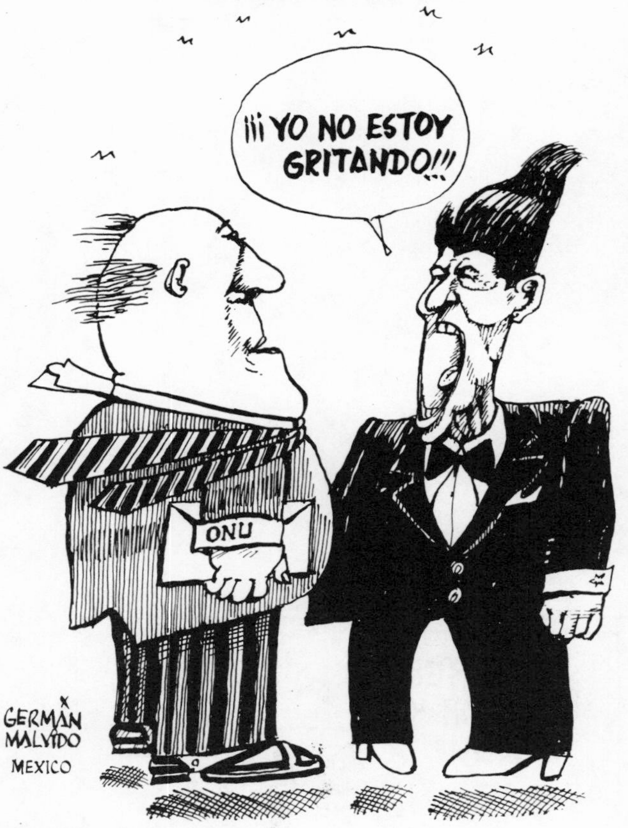
¡¡¡YO NO ESTOY GRITANDO!!!
ONU
GERMÁN MALVIDO
MEXICO

CARLOS B. MALVIDO
Mexico

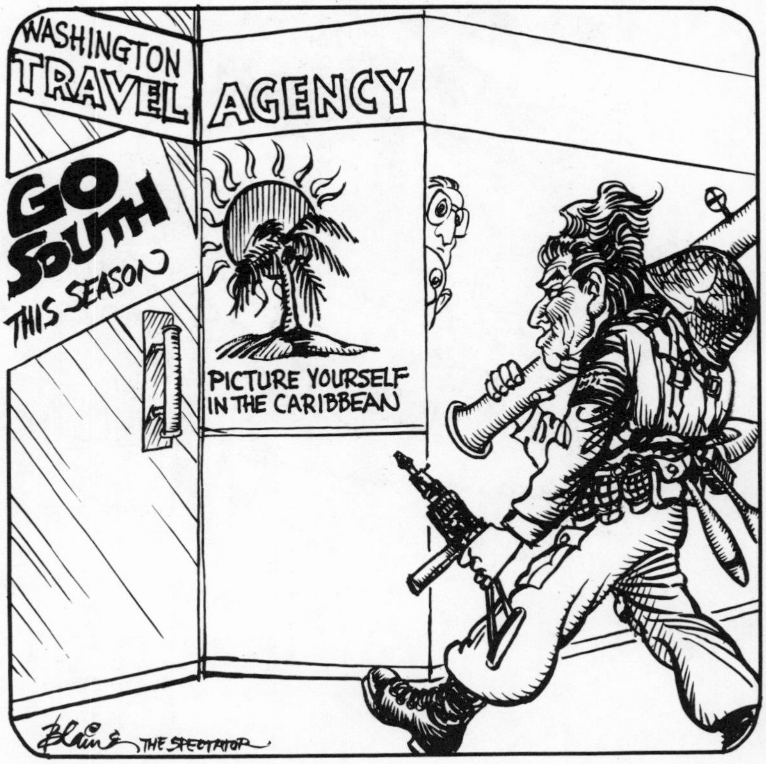
WASHINGTON TRAVEL AGENCY
GO SOUTH THIS SEASON
PICTURE YOURSELF IN THE CARIBBEAN
THE SPECTATOR

BLAINE
Courtesy Hamilton (Ont.) Spectator

JIMMY MARGULIES
©Rothco

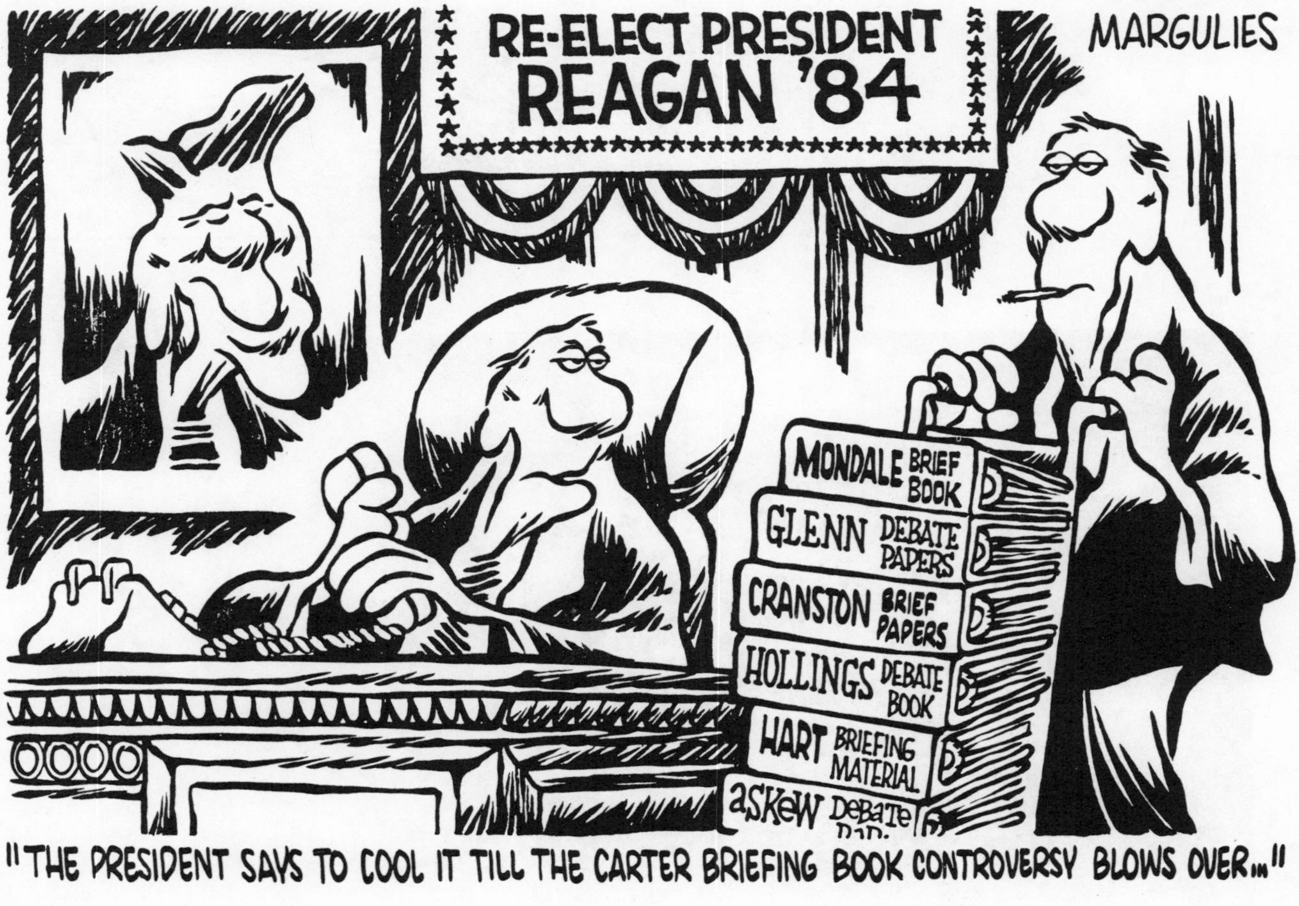
MARGULIES
RE-ELECT PRESIDENT REAGAN '84
MONDALE BRIEF BOOK
GLENN DEBATE PAPERS
CRANSTON BRIEF PAPERS
HOLLINGS DEBATE BOOK
HART BRIEFING MATERIAL
ASKEW DEBATE
"THE PRESIDENT SAYS TO COOL IT TILL THE CARTER BRIEFING BOOK CONTROVERSY BLOWS OVER..."

CAT ON A HOT TIN ROOF

JACK JURDEN
*Courtesy Wilmington Evening
Journal–News*

ART HENRIKSON
©Paddock Publications

CHARLES BISSELL
Courtesy The Tennessean

"Can't Figure Why They Don't Know What To Call It"

Democratic Hopefuls

The two leading contenders for the Democratic presidential nomination, Walter Mondale and John Glenn, attacked each other in forums and in the press during the latter part of the year. Glenn, whose campaign had been slipping, portrayed Mondale as anti-defense and as a big spender on social programs. Mondale, who received the endorsement of organized labor, teachers, and other special interest groups, charged Glenn with offering the Pentagon a blank check and with being a supporter of Reaganomics.

The Reverend Jesse Jackson rattled both parties in his quest for the presidency. Jackson captivated the news media, and his candidacy apparently encouraged blacks to register to vote by the tens of thousands.

The remaining candidates appeared at year's end to be virtually out of the running. They were California Senator Alan Cranston, former Florida Governor Reuben Askew, South Carolina Senator Ernest F. Hollings, Colorado Senator Gary Hart, and former South Dakota Senator George McGovern.

Glenn was expected to be aided by the release of *The Right Stuff*, a movie about the seven original U.S. astronauts, but widespread support did not materialize. Mondale's association with the Carter administration seemed to be a personal albatross.

GENE BASSET
Courtesy Atlanta Journal

KIRK WALTERS
Courtesy Scranton Times

JACK BENDER
Courtesy Waterloo Courier

JEFF MACNELLY
Courtesy Chicago Tribune

22

TOM CURTIS
Courtesy Milwaukee Sentinel

"The right stuff!"

BOB TAYLOR
Courtesy Dallas Times–Herald

REV. JESSE JACKSON

KAL © 1983
THE ECONOMIST
LONDON, ENGLAND

KEVIN KALLAUGHER
Courtesy London (U.K.) Observer

JACK OHMAN
Courtesy The Oregonian

OHMAN THE OREGONIAN © 1983 BY THE TRIBUNE COMPANY

CRAIG MACINTOSH
Courtesy Minneapolis Star–Tribune

JERRY BARNETT
Courtesy Indianapolis News

KIRK WALTERS
Courtesy Scranton Times

KIRK R. TINGBLAD
College Press Service

—And everywhere that Walter went—

JON KENNEDY
Courtesy Arkansas Democrat

HY ROSEN
Courtesy Albany Times–Union

U.S. Foreign Policy

President Reagan's foreign policy, based on speaking and acting from strength, came under considerable criticism during the year. His decision to send U.S. Marines to Lebanon as part of a multinational peacekeeping force was questioned in many quarters. When a bomb-laden truck driven by a terrorist crashed into marine headquarters, killing 239 persons, a mounting chorus demanded their withdrawal.

In Central America, Reagan had followed a policy of aiding those who were fighting leftist governments or guerrillas. Congress had provided some aid in that direction, but Reagan pressed for more. The president's bold move in Grenada seemed to signal to Castro that fomenting revolution in Central America would be more costly for him. The U.S. mission to rescue the tiny Caribbean island that had been taken over by leftist forces received the general approval from the American public and Congress. Even Democratic House Speaker Tip O'Neill reluctantly and belatedly agreed it was probably the proper course of action.

The U.S. continued to aid the government of El Salvador, which was fighting to survive heightening leftist guerrilla threat, and channeled assistance to rebels opposing the leftist Sandinista government of Nicaragua. The U.S. also staged large-scale maneuvers in Honduras as a show of force.

DAVID HORSEY
Courtesy Seattle Post–Intelligencer

PAUL CONRAD
Courtesy Los Angeles Times

PAUL SZEP
Courtesy Boston Globe

" PLAY IT AGAIN, RON..."

"SPEAK SOFTLY AND CARRY A BIG SHTIK ..."

STEVE SACK
Courtesy Minneapolis Tribune

THE IMPROVISER

V. CULLUM ROGERS
Courtesy Durham Morning Herald

DAVID SATTLER
*Courtesy Lafayette (Ind.) Journal and
Courier*

"OUT OF THE MOTHBALLS"

JACK OHMAN
Courtesy The Oregonian

HIS

MIKE PETERS
Courtesy Dayton Daily News

REAGAN DIPLOMATIC CORPS

FOREIGN SERVICE OFFICER

TIMOTHY ATSEFF
Courtesy Syracuse Herald-Journal

TOM FLOYD
Courtesy Indiana Post-Tribune

KAL 007

On September 1, Korean Airlines Flight 007 was shot down by a Soviet fighter plane, killing all 269 passengers aboard, including Georgia Congressman Larry McDonald. The Boeing 747 airliner had stopped in Anchorage, Alaska, for refueling en route to Seoul, Korea, and later accidentally strayed into Russian airspace.

Intelligence information revealed that the Russians had tracked the aircraft on radar for at least two and a half hours, and that more than one Soviet fighter had made visual contact. At least one had observed the 747 for some fourteen minutes before the attack.

The Russians at first denied the incident had occurred. When tapes of the Soviet pilots' conversations were released by Japanese monitoring stations, however, the Russians acknowledged the deed, claiming that KAL 007 was a spy plane. In addition to Congressman McDonald, sixty other Americans and ten Canadians were among the dead.

The world expressed outrage over the callous act, and the Soviet Union was soundly condemned. The U.S. demanded an offical apology and payment to relatives of the dead. The Soviets offered neither.

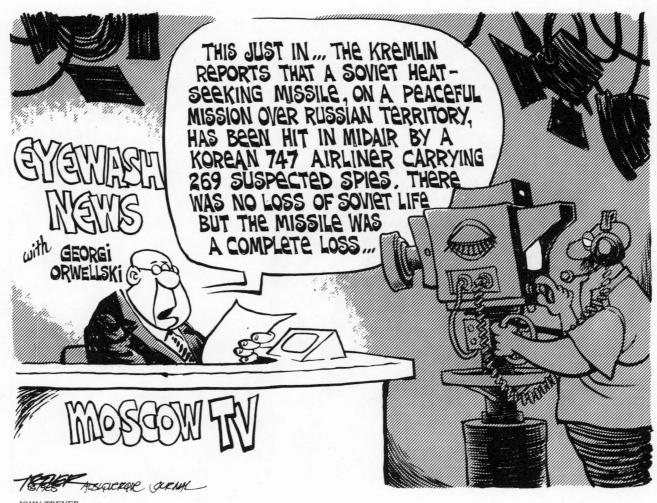

JOHN TREVER
Courtesy Albuquerque Journal

WAYNE STAYSKAL
Courtesy Chicago Tribune

RUSSIAN PILOTS SCRAMBLE TO CHECK ANOTHER PLANE REPORTED IN SOVIET AIRSPACE.

RAY OSRIN
Courtesy Cleveland Plain Dealer

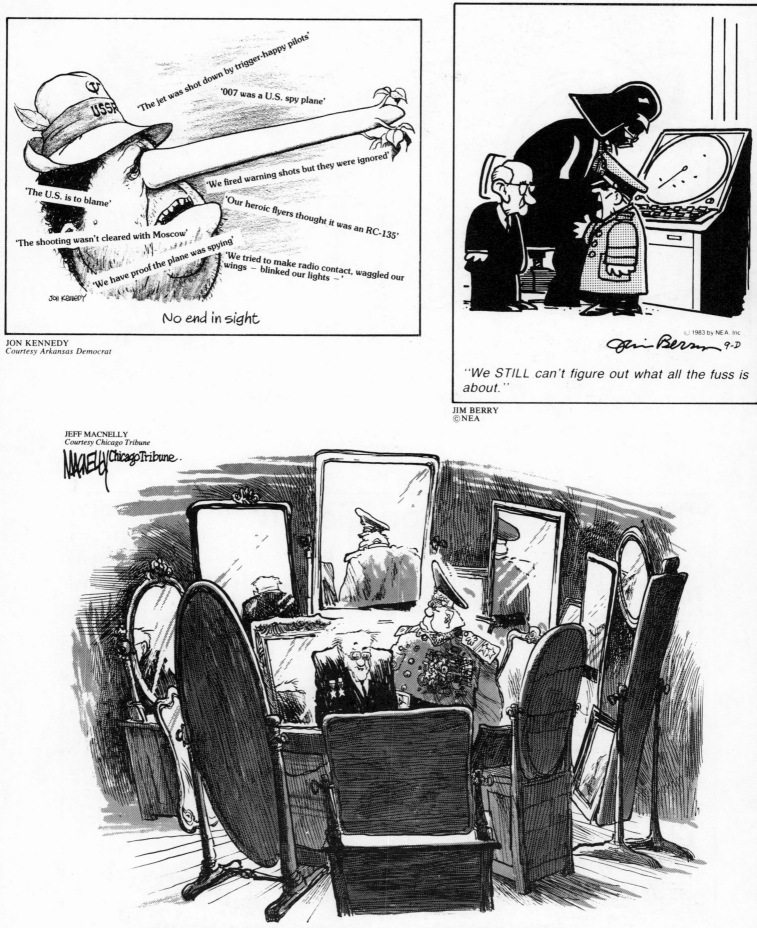

'The jet was shot down by trigger-happy pilots'

'007 was a U.S. spy plane'

'We fired warning shots but they were ignored'

'The U.S. is to blame'

'Our heroic flyers thought it was an RC-135'

'The shooting wasn't cleared with Moscow'

'We have proof the plane was spying'

'We tried to make radio contact, waggled our wings – blinked our lights –'

No end in sight

JON KENNEDY
Courtesy Arkansas Democrat

"We STILL can't figure out what all the fuss is about."

JIM BERRY
©NEA

JEFF MACNELLY
Courtesy Chicago Tribune

"We are surrounded by dangerous paranoids, Comrade. – Call in an air strike!!"

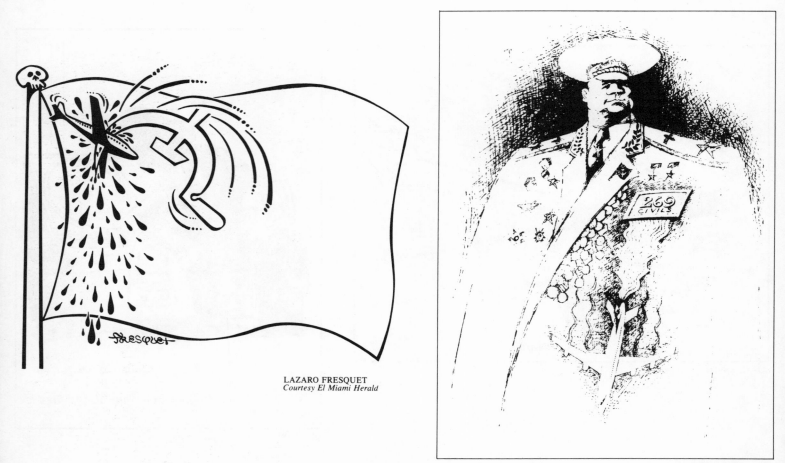

LAZARO FRESQUET
Courtesy El Miami Herald

LOUIS MITLBERG
Courtesy L'Express (France)

BOB GORRELL
Courtesy Richmond News

JACK JURDEN
*Courtesy Wilmington Evening
Journal–News*

BARBARIC

EDDIE GERMANO
Courtesy Brockton Daily Enterprise

TOM ENGELHARDT
Courtesy St. Louis Post–Dispatch

'The Airliner Was A Snap, Comrade Marshal —
Shooting Down The Truth Will Be A Little Harder'

From Out Of The Blue . . . Red

TOM CURTIS
Courtesy Milwaukee Sentinel

"The US made me do it!"

"Ah-hah. . . unarmed and innocent airline passengers posing as unarmed and innocent airline passengers!"

BILL GRAHAM
Courtesy Arkansas Gazette

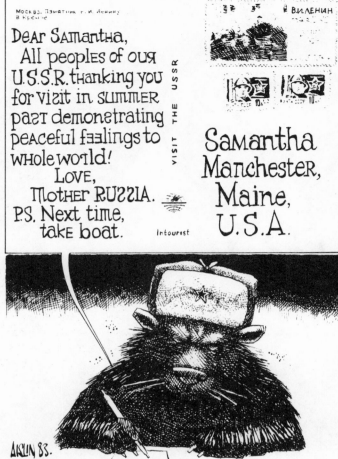

TERRY MOSHER (AISLIN)
Courtesy Montreal Gazette

KIRK R. TINGBLAD
College Press Service

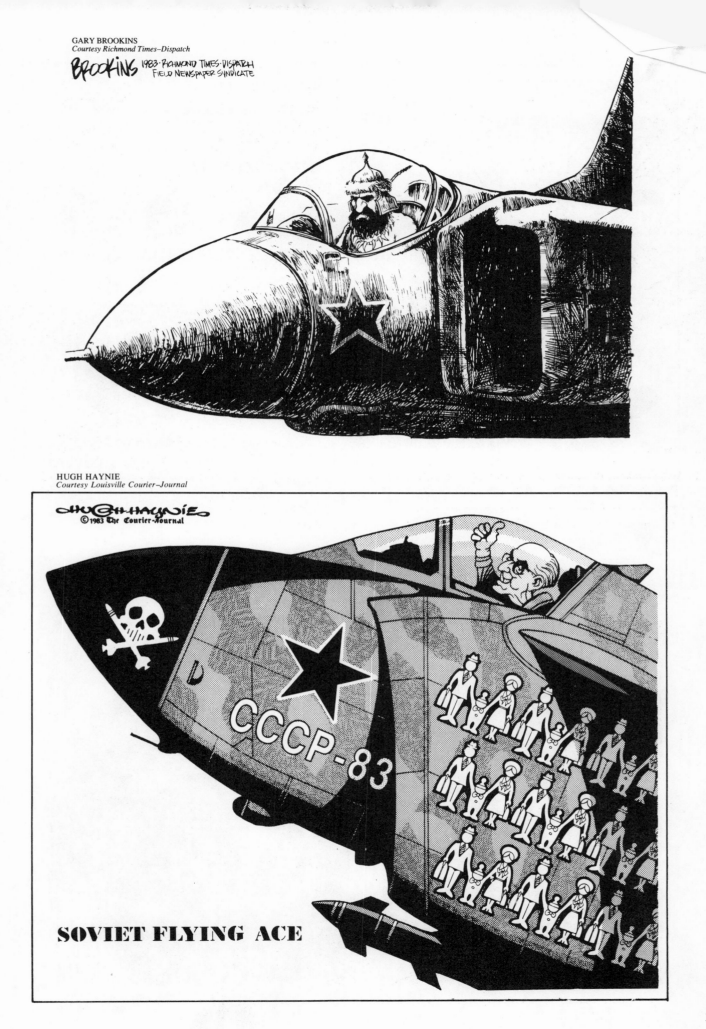

BROOKINS 1983·RICHMOND·TIMES·DISPATCH
FIELD NEWSPAPER SYNDICATE

HUGH HAYNIE
©1983 The Courier-Journal

CCCP-83

SOVIET FLYING ACE

JOHN CRAWFORD
Courtesy Alabama Journal

DICK LOCHER
Courtesy Chicago Tribune

WALT HANDELSMAN
Courtesy Catonville Times

LARRY WRIGHT
Courtesy Detroit News

JOHN R. THORNTON
Courtesy Republican Journal

MERLE TINGLEY
Courtesy London Free Press (Can.)

"Stumblebum Or Not, Ivan, I Don't Know What I'd Do Without You!"

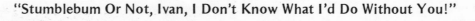

CHARLES BISSELL
Courtesy The Tennessean

Grenada

In a coup on October 19, Prime Minister Maurice Bishop and a number of high-ranking government officials were assassinated. Control of the country was grabbed by General Hudson Austin, head of the armed forces and a self-proclaimed hard-line leftist.

U.S. Navy ships were dispatched to the area, and President Reagan expressed concern for the safety of some one thousand U.S. citizens on the island, most of them students at Grenada's small medical school. An assault force of 1,900 U.S. Marines and airborne troops landed on the island on October 25. They were joined by forces from several of the surrounding Caribbean nations. It had been suspected that Cuba had been working to convert Grenada into a Soviet-Cuban colony. Huge stores of arms were uncovered, and secret military aid agreements between the island government and Soviet-bloc nations were disclosed.

The American public—with the notable exception of the Democratic presidential candidates—showed widespread support for the U.S. action. Journalists complained about restrictions imposed by the U.S. military on news coverage of the conflict.

By November 2 hostilities had ceased, order was restored, and the coup's leaders were jailed.

JUST FOR THE RECORD

FRANK EVERS
Courtesy New York Daily News

DRAWING THE LINE

← GRENADA

CHUCK ASAY
Courtesy Colorado Springs Sun

"We're lucky Ronald Reagan wasn't president at the time of the Bay of Pigs, eh, comrade?"

JIM BERRY
©NEA

WE WERE INVITED...

AFGHANISTAN

GRENADA

BOB ENGLEHART
Courtesy Hartford Courant

42

BILL GARNER
Courtesy Washington Times

JOHN MILT MORRIS
©The Associated Press

HY ROSEN
Courtesy Albany Times–Union

ED FISCHER
Courtesy Rochester Post–Bulletin

DICK WALLMEYER
Courtesy Independent Press–Telegram
(Calif.)

JEFF MACNELLY
Courtesy Chicago Tribune

ENEMY WEAPONS CACHE SEIZED ON GRENADA—*news item...*

IN THE NAME OF SAFETY

"NOW, IF YOU'LL COOPERATE — I'LL GIVE YOU AN INSTANT ANALYSIS
OF THESE PROBLEMS AND HOW TO SOLVE THEM!"

JON KENNEDY
Courtesy Arkansas Democrat

All the right moves

MIKE SHELTON
Courtesy Santa Ana Register

JOHN DEERING
Courtesy Arkansas Democrat

GARY BROOKINS
Courtesy Richmond Times–Dispatch

"...REGARDING THIS SO-CALLED RESCUE MISSION, MR. WOODSMAN.... WE FIND NO EVIDENCE THAT GRANDMA AND MS. RIDING HOOD WERE IN IMMINENT DANGER!... WE DEPLORE THIS UNLAWFUL INTRUSION INTO AN INTERNAL AFFAIR!!...."

DICK WALLMEYER
Courtesy Independent Press–Telegram
(Calif.)

EDGAR (SOL) SOLLER
Courtesy California Examiner

GENE BASSET
Courtesy Atlanta Journal

"WE'RE JUST PROTECTING YOU FROM REPORTING A BUM STORY."

Arms Race

Discussions concerning a possible arms control agreement with the Soviet Union continued throughout 1983. In 1981 President Reagan had offered a "zero option" plan that would have required the Russians to remove their intermediate-range missiles from Europe in exchange for a halt to U.S. plans to deploy Pershing II and cruise missiles. In March of 1983 Reagan submitted a new proposal that would have given each side the same number of missiles in Europe. Two other Reagan proposals—the first giving each adversary an equal number of nuclear warheads and the other suggesting an absolute limit of 420 warheads—were, like his earlier plans, firmly rejected by the Soviets.

Many church groups during the year issued statements favoring some type of nuclear disarmament. In May, the Catholic bishops of America ratified a pastoral letter condemning nuclear weapons and stating that no situation would ever justify their use.

In November, ABC-TV touched off a national furor with the showing of the movie "The Day After," a version of what would supposedly happen if nuclear war came. Much discussion of the merits of the program and the intent of its creators followed, but apparently the show failed to rally new supporters to the nuclear freeze movement.

MIKE PETERS
Courtesy Dayton Daily News

NOW I'LL NEVER GET BACK TO KANSAS...

BOB RICH
Courtesy New Haven Register

The Day After.

 ELDON PLETCHER
Courtesy New Orleans Times–Picayune

"NOW THAT WE'VE AGREED ON REDUCTION OF WARHEADS, LET'S TALK ABOUT MISSILES."

AUNTIE NUKE AND UNCLE SAM

MERLE TINGLEY
Courtesy London Free Press (Can.)

JOHN MILT MORRIS
©The Associated Press

H. CLAY BENNETT
Courtesy St. Petersburg Times

52

LEE JUDGE
Courtesy Kansas City Times

DISARMAMENT TALKS

DICK WALLMEYER
Courtesy Independent Press–Telegram
(Calif.)

CHUCK AYERS
Courtesy Akron Beacon–Journal

KEVIN KALLAUGHER
© K.K. Syndication Service (Eng.)

LOUIS MITLBERG
Courtesy L'Express (France)

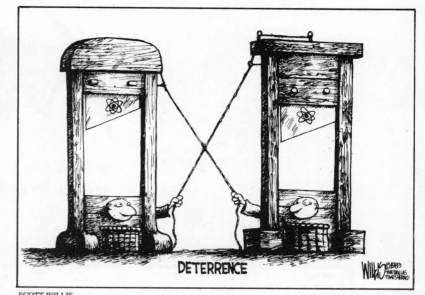

DETERRENCE

SCOTT WILLIS
Courtesy Dallas Times–Herald

DAVID HORSEY
Courtesy Seattle Post–Intelligencer

BOB RICH
Courtesy New Haven Register

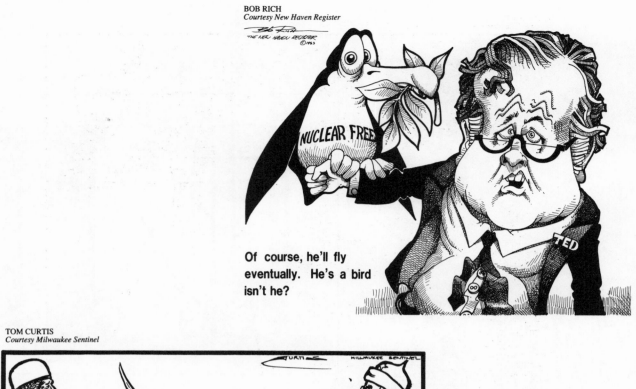

Of course, he'll fly
eventually. He's a bird
isn't he?

TOM CURTIS
Courtesy Milwaukee Sentinel

"He's threatening to attack my sword with a shield!"

MIKE MORGAN
Courtesy Macon Telegraph & News

BILL GARNER
Courtesy Washington Times

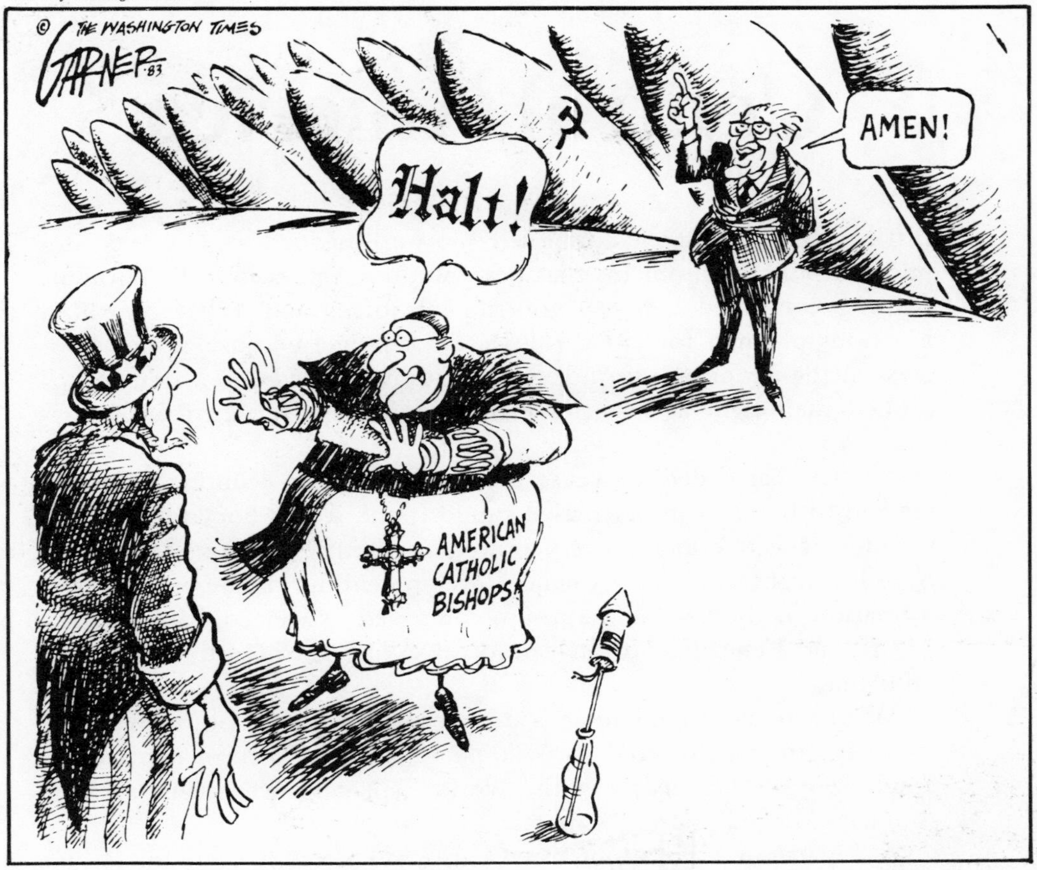

© THE WASHINGTON TIMES
GARNER '83
Halt!
AMEN!
AMERICAN CATHOLIC BISHOPS

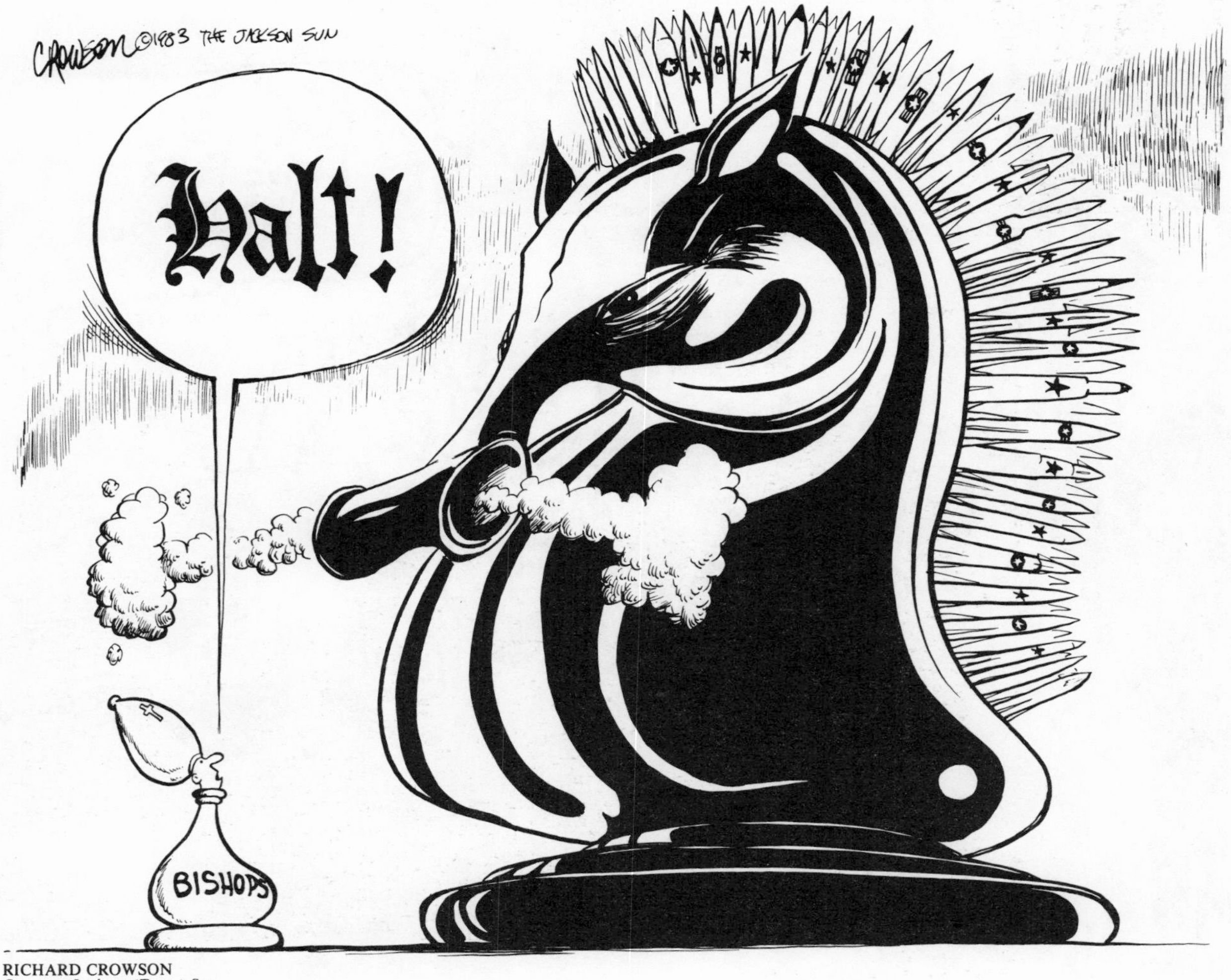

CROWSON ©1983 THE JACKSON SUN
Halt!
BISHOPS

RICHARD CROWSON
Courtesy Jackson (Tenn.) Sun

Central America

Little progress was made during 1983 toward solving the massive economic and political problems that beset Central America. In El Salvador, fighting continued between government forces and leftist guerrillas. Elections planned for late 1983 were postponed because of slow progress in the adoption of a new constitution. Armed opposition groups pushed their fight against the leftist Sandinista government in Nicaragua.

As the year ended, however, efforts to promote economic stability seemed to be receiving increased support, and it was hoped that as the world-wide economic recovery moved forward, conditions in Central America might improve. A major development during the year was the formation of the Contadora group, composed of Mexico, Panama, Colombia, and Venezuela, to seek peaceful solutions to Central American problems.

Mexico remained mired in a deep economic crisis, but a sweeping austerity program offered some hope for relief. Foreign debts once again were rescheduled, and the World Bank approved loans to help stimulate Mexico's non-oil exports.

A bipartisan commission on Central America, headed by Henry Kissinger, was appointed by President Reagan at mid-year. The commission was charged with reviewing the entire problem of Central America and making recommendations.

THE ORLANDO SENTINEL

ALEJO VAZONEZ LIRA
Mexico

DRAPER HILL
Courtesy Detroit News

BOB GORRELL
Courtesy Richmond News

59

WALT HANDELSMAN
Courtesy Catonville Times

TOM DARCY
Courtesy Newsday

MEANWHILE IN OUR OWN BACKYARD

JIM LANGE
Courtesy Daily Oklahoman

TOM TOLES
Courtesy Buffalo News

H. CLAY BENNETT
Courtesy St. Petersburg Times

TOM MEYER
Courtesy San Francisco Chronicle

JIMMY MARGULIES
© Rothco

ELDON PLETCHER
Courtesy New Orleans Times–Picayune

EDD ULUSCHAK
Courtesy Edmonton Journal

BRIAN BASSET
Courtesy Seattle Times

ETTA HULME
Courtesy Ft. Worth Star–Telegram

"The U.S. State Department has again certified that growing numbers of El Salvadorans have been placed in positions where their human rights will no longer be violated...."

AL LIEDERMAN
©Rothco

ROTHCO

JIM BORGMAN
Courtesy Cincinnati Enquirer

CHAN LOWE
Courtesy Oklahoma City Times

CONTINUING PRISONERS OF THE VIETNAM WAR.

STEVE GREENBERG
Courtesy Los Angeles Daily News

MILT PRIGGEE
Courtesy Dayton Journal–Herald

MIKE KEEFE
Courtesy Denver Post

Middle East

In Lebanon, the civil war that began in 1975 flared anew, with Palestinian, Moslem, Druse, and Christian forces fighting each other and the Lebanese army as well. About 98 percent of the country's land area was occupied by foreign forces and private militias. Centuries-old feuds added to the strife as various factions used frequent bombings and hit-and-run tactics.

The United Nations multinational peacekeeping force became a constant target of terrorists around Beirut. On April 18 a vehicle loaded with explosives was driven to the U.S. embassy and detonated. More than 60 persons were killed and 100 wounded. Then, on October 23, a truck filled with six tons of TNT crashed through barriers and slammed into the U.S. Marine headquarters. The resulting explosion and collapse of the building killed 241 marines. It was one of the blackest days in American military history. Less than two minutes after the blast at marine headquarters, another truck, similarly loaded, blew up a French barracks, killing 58 paratroopers.

The year saw two familiar faces leave the scene as political powers. Israeli Prime Minister Menachem Begin resigned from office, and Yasir Arafat was forced to flee Beirut by mutineers in his own Palestine Liberation Organization. The mutineers were backed by Syrian forces.

SANDY CAMPBELL
Courtesy The Tennessean

MIKE GRASTON
Courtesy Windsor Star (Ont.)

BILL GARNER
Courtesy Washington Times

SIGNE WILKINSON
Courtesy San Jose Mercury–News

JERRY ROBINSON
©Cartoonists & Writers Syndicate

BRIAN BASSET
Courtesy Seattle Times

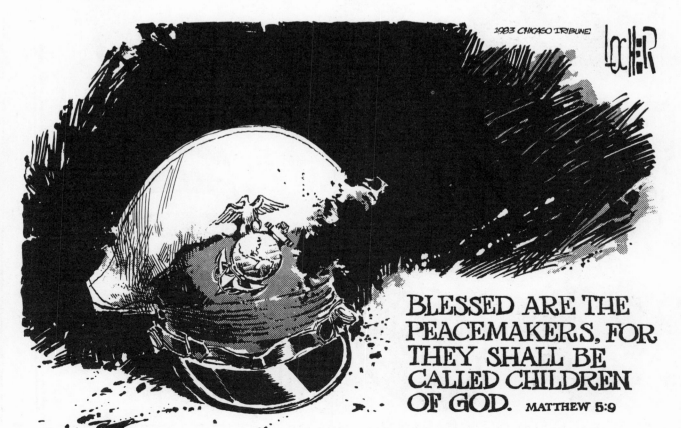

DICK LOCHER
Courtesy Chicago Tribune

MIKE KEEFE
Courtesy Denver Post

JACK MCLEOD
Courtesy Times–Journal Co. (D.C.)

HY ROSEN
Courtesy Albany Times–Union

JACK JURDEN
*Courtesy Wilmington Evening
Journal–News*

BIGGER ROLE IN BEIRUT

CRAIG MACINTOSH
Courtesy Minneapolis Star–Tribune

JIM BERRY
©NEA

"WONDER HOW MUCH LONGER WE'LL BE HERE "KEEPING THE PEACE"?"

VERN THOMPSON
Courtesy Lawton (Okla.) Constitution

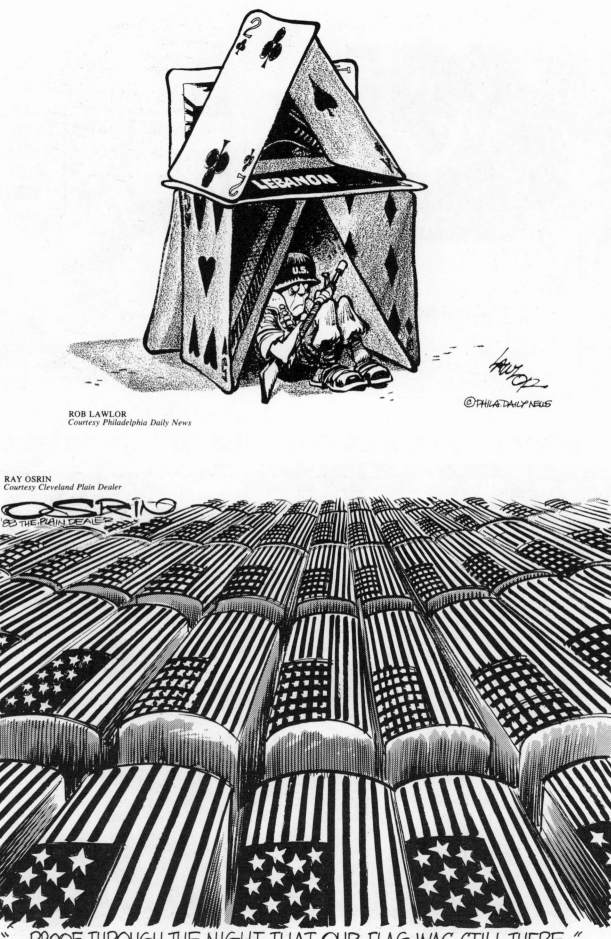

ROB LAWLOR
Courtesy Philadelphia Daily News

RAY OSRIN
Courtesy Cleveland Plain Dealer

"...PROOF THROUGH THE NIGHT THAT OUR FLAG WAS STILL THERE."

TOM DARCY
Courtesy Newsday

STEVE KELLEY
Courtesy San Diego Union

73

GENE BASSET
©United Features Syndicate

RICHARD ALLISON
Courtesy Army Times

ART BIMROSE
Courtesy The Oregonian

DANA SUMMERS
Courtesy Orlando Sentinel

BERT WHITMAN
Courtesy Phoenix Gazette

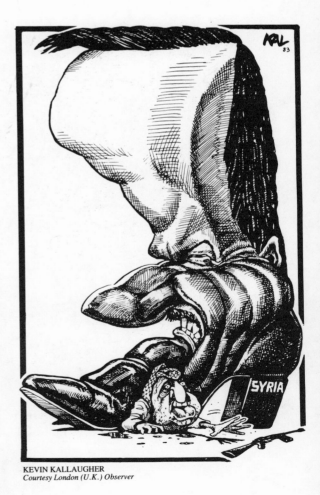

KEVIN KALLAUGHER
Courtesy London (U.K.) Observer

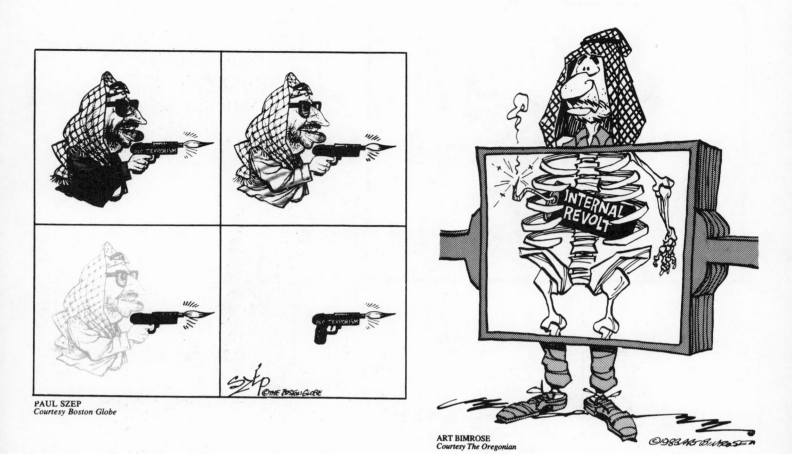

PAUL SZEP
Courtesy Boston Globe

ART BIMROSE
Courtesy The Oregonian

"Okay . . . get the car bomb ready! There
it is! The U. S. Embassy!"

HUGH HAYNIE
Courtesy Louisville Courier–Journal

ED GAMBLE
Courtesy Florida Times–Union

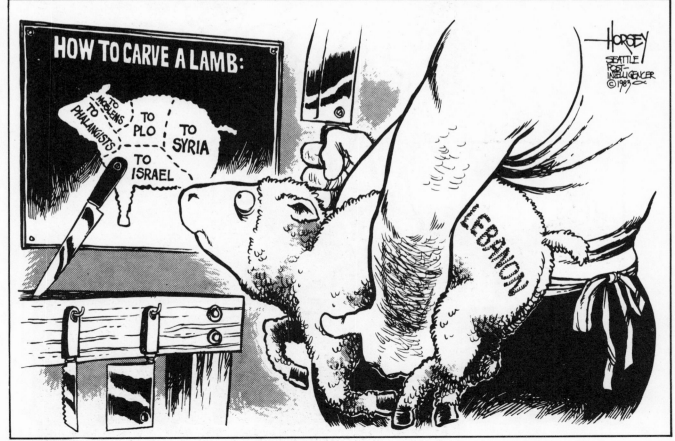

DAVID HORSEY
Courtesy Seattle Post–Intelligencer

THE OFFICIAL GUIDE TO MID-EAST PEACE...

START

FINISH

JEFF KOTERBA
Courtesy Papillion (Neb.) Times

MID EAST GAS

ANDROPOV

BILL MITCHELL
Courtesy American Politics

LEBANON

BEUTEL
TELEGRAPH-
JOURNAL

JOSH BEUTEL
Courtesy St. John Telegraph-Journal

Foreign Affairs

Poland continued to experience political and economic turmoil, as the inept government of General Wojciech Jaruzelski seemed unable to solve the problems facing the beleaguered country. Although the independent trade union Solidarity remained banned, its leader, Lech Walesa, was awarded the Nobel Peace Prize for 1983.

A high point for the year for many Poles was the visit of Pope John Paul II to his homeland. While in Poland the pope criticized the repressiveness of the military government and called for more freedom for the people.

Russian leader Yuri Andropov, in a public relations move, invited 11-year-old Samantha Smith of Maine to visit the Soviet Union. The youngster had written Andropov expressing her opposition to nuclear war, and the ailing Russian leader cleverly fit her into his propaganda machine.

Buoyed by a rising economy and the British military victory in the Falkland Islands, British Prime Minister Margaret Thatcher called an election for June 9. She buried the Labor Party opposition in the most impressive electoral victory in Britain since 1945.

Philippines President Ferdinand Marcos clung to power by the tightest of margins following the public assassination of opposition leader Benigno Aquino, Jr. The belief that the government was involved in the assassination was so widespread that Marcos found it necessary to deny the rumors on national television. Many of his countrymen, however, remained unconvinced.

JON KENNEDY
Courtesy Arkansas Democrat

1990

GENE BASSET
Courtesy Atlanta Journal

SUPPORT

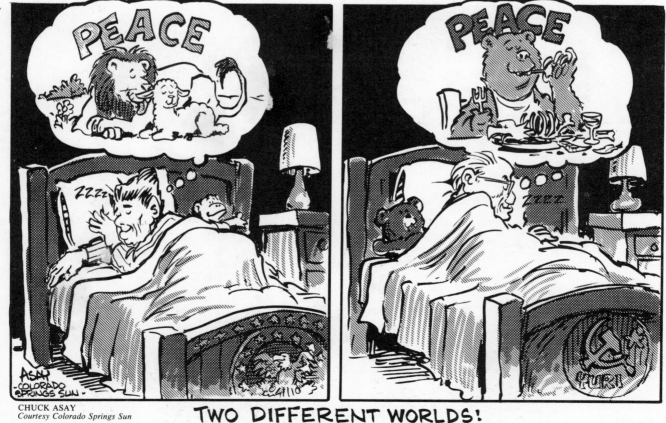

CHUCK ASAY
Courtesy Colorado Springs Sun

TWO DIFFERENT WORLDS!

80

JERRY ROBINSON
©Cartoonists & Writers Syndicate

JIM MORGAN
Courtesy Spartanburg Herald-Journal

BRIAN BASSET
Courtesy Seattle Times

LOUIS MITLBERG
Courtesy L'Express (France)

MILT PRIGGEE
Courtesy Dayton Journal–Herald

DRAPER HILL
Courtesy Detroit News

'You Can't Spell Your Name...
And You Can't Keep Your Mouth Shut!'

EDDIE GERMANO
Courtesy Brockton Daily Enterprise

STEVE KELLEY
Courtesy San Diego Union

83

MIKE GRASTON
Courtesy Windsor Star (Ont.)

KIRK WALTERS
Courtesy Scranton Times

EDMUND VALTMAN
© Rothco

A MESSAGE FROM THE OUTSIDE

84

SOVIET AIR SPACE VIOLATED

JIM LANGE
Courtesy Daily Oklahoman

BILL SANDERS
Courtesy Milwaukee Journal

GEORGE DANBY
Courtesy New Haven Register

ED STEIN
Courtesy Rocky Mountain News

MERLE TINGLEY
Courtesy London Free Press (Can.)

Economy

The economic picture brightened across the United States in 1983 after a painful period of recession. The recovery was sparked by two factors—a continued low rate of inflation and a drop in interest rates. The prime rate dropped to a low of 10.5 percent, and the inflation rate was an almost imperceptible 2.9 percent.

The auto and housing industries led the way in the recovery. Housing starts for the year were up 45 percent, while auto sales were the best since 1979. Unemployment declined from a peak of 10.8 percent in 1982 to 8.2 percent at the end of 1983. A record 102.7 million Americans held jobs, and plants began recalling laid-off workers and investing in new equipment.

The breakup of American Telephone and Telegraph was concluded with final divestiture on January 1, 1984. AT&T retained control of its long-distance lines, its manufacturing subsidiary, and some laboratories. For the consumer, the net result was higher telephone rates.

In August, 675,000 workers went on strike against AT&T. The shutdown lasted 16 days before an agreement was reached. Then, in November, Greyhound was hit by a strike after asking its employees to take a 9.5 percent pay cut to aid the company through difficult financial times. Agreement was reached at the end of the month, with workers making substantial concessions.

BROOKINS RICHMOND TIMES-DISPATCH ©1983 FIELD ENTERPRISES, INC.

GARY BROOKINS
Courtesy Richmond Times–Dispatch

CHARLES DANIEL
Courtesy Knoxville Journal

BOB GORRELL
Courtesy Richmond News

CHUCK ASAY
Courtesy Colorado Springs Sun

DICK LOCHER
Courtesy Chicago Tribune

1983 CHICAGO TRIBUNE

RAY OSRIN
Courtesy Cleveland Plain Dealer

OUR NEW BILLING GUIDELINES

JOHN DEERING
Courtesy Arkansas Democrat

ETTA HULME
Courtesy Ft. Worth Star–Telegram

LAMBERT DER
Courtesy Raleigh Times

COLLECTIVE BARGAINING....UNION STYLE

VERN THOMPSON
Courtesy Lawton (Okla.) Constitution

MIKE PETERS
Courtesy Dayton Daily News

EDD ULUSCHAK
Courtesy Edmonton Journal

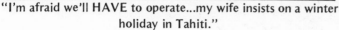

"I'm afraid we'll HAVE to operate...my wife insists on a winter holiday in Tahiti."

TOM TOLES
Courtesy Buffalo News

JOHN CRAWFORD
Courtesy Alabama Journal

JERRY BARNETT
Courtesy Indianapolis News

AL LIEDERMAN
©Rothco

JACK BENDER
Courtesy Waterloo Courier

JERRY BARNETT
Courtesy Indianapolis News

JOSEPH HELLER
Courtesy West Bend News (Wisc.)

THE HORNS OF A DILEMMA...

STEVE LINDSTROM
Courtesy Duluth News–Tribune

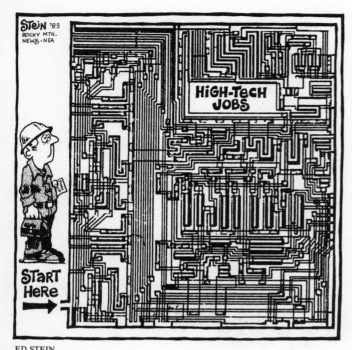

ED STEIN
Courtesy Rocky Mountain News

BERT WHITMAN
Courtesy Phoenix Gazette

ED ASHLEY
Courtesy Toledo Blade

JACK MCLEOD
Courtesy Times–Journal Co. (D.C.)

©1983 FEDERAL TIMES

'...OH, YOU NOTICED THE DIFFERENCE WHEN MY WATCHDOG BARKS AT ME...'

JIM PALMER
Courtesy Montgomery Advertiser

STEVE SACK
Courtesy Minneapolis Tribune

DAVID SATTLER
*Courtesy Lafayette (Ind.) Journal and
    Courier*

Crime

As in previous years, heavy traffic in drugs plagued the U.S. in 1983. The careers of several well-known professional football players were clouded by drug charges, and professional baseball came under scrutiny. There were numerous probes into drug use, even on Capitol Hill in Washington. Three lawmakers were named as targets. The trio denied the charges and, after an investigation, the Justice Department announced that there was insufficient evidence for indictments. The congressional ethics committee, however, decided to continue its inquiry.

As more and more people bought personal computers, the risk of unauthorized individuals' tapping into government, business, or academic computer systems has continued to grow. Among bright young computer buffs, such computer tapping has become regarded as something of a sport. Several startling cases of computer break-ins have pointed to the need to improve computer security.

Drunk driving continued as a national tragedy; according to police authorities, it accounts for at least half of the 50,000 highway fatalities each year. The legal age for drinking was raised in some states in 1983, and in several states drunken drivers involved in fatal accidents were charged with murder.

The U.S. prison population continued to soar in 1983, reaching a record high of 431,829 inmates by mid-year.

STAYSKAL
83 CHICAGO
TRIBUNE

LIFE EXPECTANCY IN THE U.S. IS NOW AT A RECORD 74!

"WITH A FEW MORE LOCKS MAYBE WE COULD GET IT UP TO 80!"

WAYNE STAYSKAL
Courtesy Chicago Tribune

"WHAT FOOLS THESE MORTALS BE!"

The Drunken Driver

CHUCK BROOKS
Courtesy Birmingham News

TIMOTHY ATSEFF
Courtesy Syracuse Herald-Journal

DOUG MACGREGOR
Courtesy Norwich Bulletin

"Kicking my coke habit is tough enough as it is without having to look at all these white lines on the field."

PAUL FELL
Courtesy Maverick Media

NEWS ITEM: '83 NFL SEASON BEGINS. VETERANS REPORT TO TRAINING CAMP.

DICK WALLMEYER
*Courtesy Independent Press—Telegram
(Calif.)*

"BE WITH YA IN A MINUTE, KID..."

NOT A GOOD CLIMATE FOR FOOTBALL

JACK JURDEN
*Courtesy Wilmington Evening
Journal–News*

JIM DOBBINS
Courtesy Union–Leader

They'd HAVE to have had holes in their heads....

PHIL BISSELL
Courtesy Lowell (Mass.) Sun

Courts

If one opinion of the U.S. Supreme Court in 1983 stood out as having the most far-reaching implications, it was undoubtedly the "one-house veto" case. The court ruled unconstitutional a provision of the Immigration and Nationality Act that had permitted one house of Congress to veto an executive branch decision. This ruling was expected to have sweeping effects by unleashing a flood of federal court decisions striking down other legislative veto provisions.

There was a lot of talk but no action on attempting to lighten the court's workload. More than 150 full opinions were issued during the year, some 20 percent more than two years earlier.

The court continued to tiptoe around the death penalty, still not making clear under what circumstances it would uphold death sentences. In religion, the court found nothing wrong with the Nebraska legislature's opening its sessions with a prayer by its chaplain, even though his salary is paid from public funds. Still before the court was a case concerning whether a nativity scene should be allowed on public property.

CHUCK ASAY
Courtesy Colorado Springs Sun

JIM KNUDSEN
Courtesy L.A. Tidings

CRUEL AND UNREASONABLE BURDEN

WAYNE STAYSKAL
Courtesy Chicago Tribune

"LET US ALL BOW OUR HEADS AND PRAY TO THE GREAT 'TO-WHOM-IT-MAY-CONCERN'!"

Congress

One of the major problems facing Congress in 1983 was the nation's huge budget deficit, but it did not seem to worry the lawmakers a great deal because they did absolutely nothing about it. Many in Congress, especially the Democrats, wanted new taxes to reduce a deficit that appeared to be pegged at about $200 billion for the year. President Reagan insisted on cuts in spending, but Congress only seemed willing to cut defense spending. In late October, the House approved slightly over $10 billion in cuts, but the Senate took no action.

A bipartisan commission on social security was appointed by President Reagan to seek ways to prevent the system from going bankrupt. A package was rushed through Congress and signed by the president on April 20. But, at best, it was another stopgap measure and did nothing to ensure the program's long-term solvency.

On October 19, President Reagan signed into law a bill designating the third Monday in January as a federal holiday commemorating the birthday of the Reverend Martin Luther King, Jr. Senator Jesse Helms of North Carolina had been a vocal opponent of the measure.

In November a time bomb exploded outside the Capitol office of the Senate Democratic leader, causing damage but no injuries. A terrorist group claimed responsibility, contending the blast was in protest of U.S. action in Grenada and Lebanon.

CHUCK AYERS
Courtesy Akron Beacon–Journal

BIG PRIZE FOR SOME FUTURE ARCHEOLOGIST!

JOHN MILT MORRIS
©The Associated Press

IF HE'S REALLY WORRIED — THERE'S A SIMPLE WAY OUT

CHUCK BROOKS
Courtesy Birmingham News

JERRY FEARING
*Courtesy St. Paul Dispatch–
Pioneer Press*

"NOW, THERE'S A GOOD JOB DONE!"

CHUCK BROOKS
Courtesy Birmingham News

UNEASY FEELING!

ART WOOD
Courtesy AFBF (Md.)

BRUCE BEATTIE
*Courtesy Daytona Beach
News–Journal*

"I'd like you to get rid of the federal deficit, make Social Security solvent again, and HEY, WAIT!... I haven't gotten to my third wish yet!"

ART WOOD
Courtesy AFBF (Md.)

JOHN TREVER
Courtesy Albuquerque Journal

MIKE SHELTON
Courtesy Santa Ana Register

BILL SANDERS
Courtesy Milwaukee Journal

ED ASHLEY
Courtesy Toledo Blade

'Must be nice to have a house to go to!'

DRAPER HILL
Courtesy Detroit News

ART BIMROSE
Courtesy The Oregonian

LARRY WRIGHT
Courtesy Detroit News

STEVE LINDSTROM
Courtesy Duluth News–Tribune

V. CULLUM ROGERS
Courtesy Durham Morning Herald

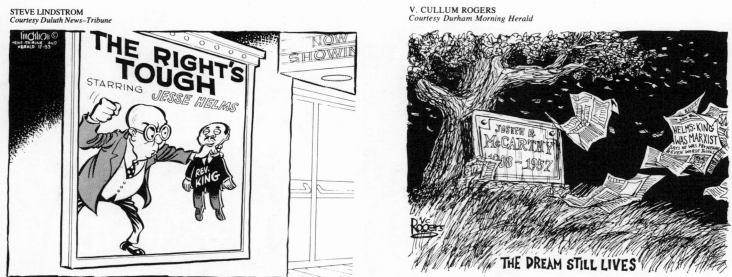

GEORGE FISHER
Courtesy Arkansas Gazette

LAMBERT DER
Courtesy Raleigh Times

SIGNE WILKINSON
Courtesy San Jose Mercury–News

JIM LANGE
Courtesy Daily Oklahoman

GEORGE FISHER
Courtesy Arkansas Gazette

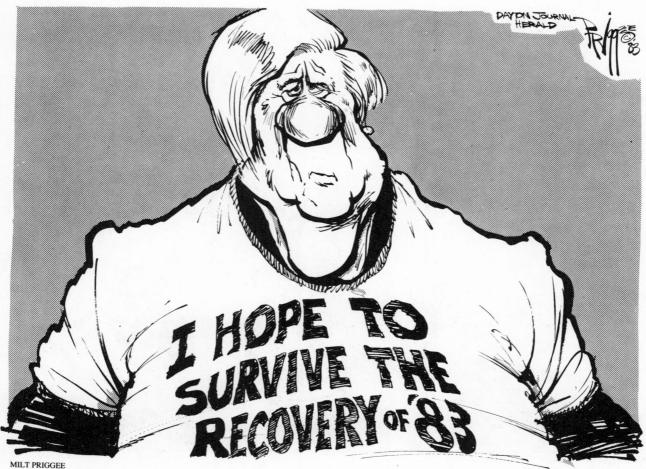

MILT PRIGGEE
Courtesy Dayton Journal–Herald

James Watt

Outspoken James Watt, one of President Reagan's original cabinet appointees, joked his way into private life from his post as secretary of the interior. A controversial, highly opinionated administrator from the beginning, Watt had drawn frequent fire from critics for his extensive leasing of federal land, as well as for his occasional intemperate remarks. In a September speech, he described a newly appointed commission as having "every kind of mix you can have. I have a black, I have a woman, two Jews, and a cripple." The insensitive remark stirred a storm of protests that did not subside until his resignation on October 9.

Watt's goal as secretary was, in his own words, "to reduce the vulnerability of America to blackmail, embargoes, or other national-security threats" by determining exactly what strategic minerals America has and how much oil is beneath government-owned lands.

His policies opened up the entire Outer Continental Shelf—nearly a billion underwater acres—to oil exploration over a five-year period. He also opened grazing lands to ranchers in the West who had clamored for years for relief from government interference in the use of vast government lands.

Watt was colorful and controversial—and an irresistible target for the nation's editorial cartoonists.

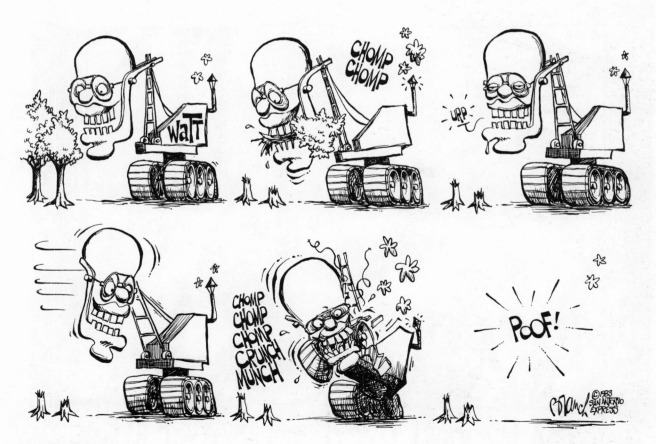

JOHN BRANCH
Courtesy San Antonio Express–News

MIKE PETERS
Courtesy Dayton Daily News

PSST, GOOD NEWS... <u>WATT'S</u> ON THE ENDANGERED SPECIES LIST.

MILT PRIGGEE
Courtesy Dayton Journal–Herald

...and they all lived happily ever after.

RANDY WICKS
Courtesy Newhall (Calif.) Signal

TIMOTHY ATSEFF
Courtesy Syracuse Herald-Journal

THE JAMES WATT MODEL

SILENCER

THE WILLIAM CLARK MODEL

STEVE GREENBERG
Courtesy Los Angeles Daily News

GARY HUCK
©Rothco

TOM MEYER
Courtesy San Francisco Chronicle

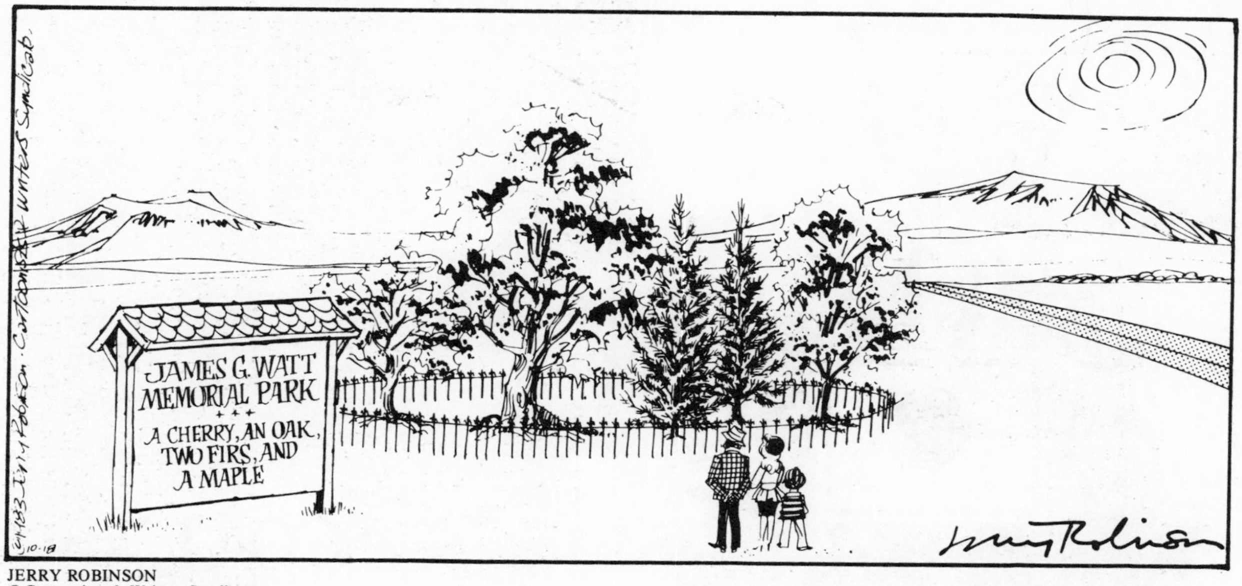
JAMES G. WATT
MEMORIAL PARK
A CHERRY, AN OAK,
TWO FIRS, AND
A MAPLE

JERRY ROBINSON
©Cartoonists & Writers Syndicate

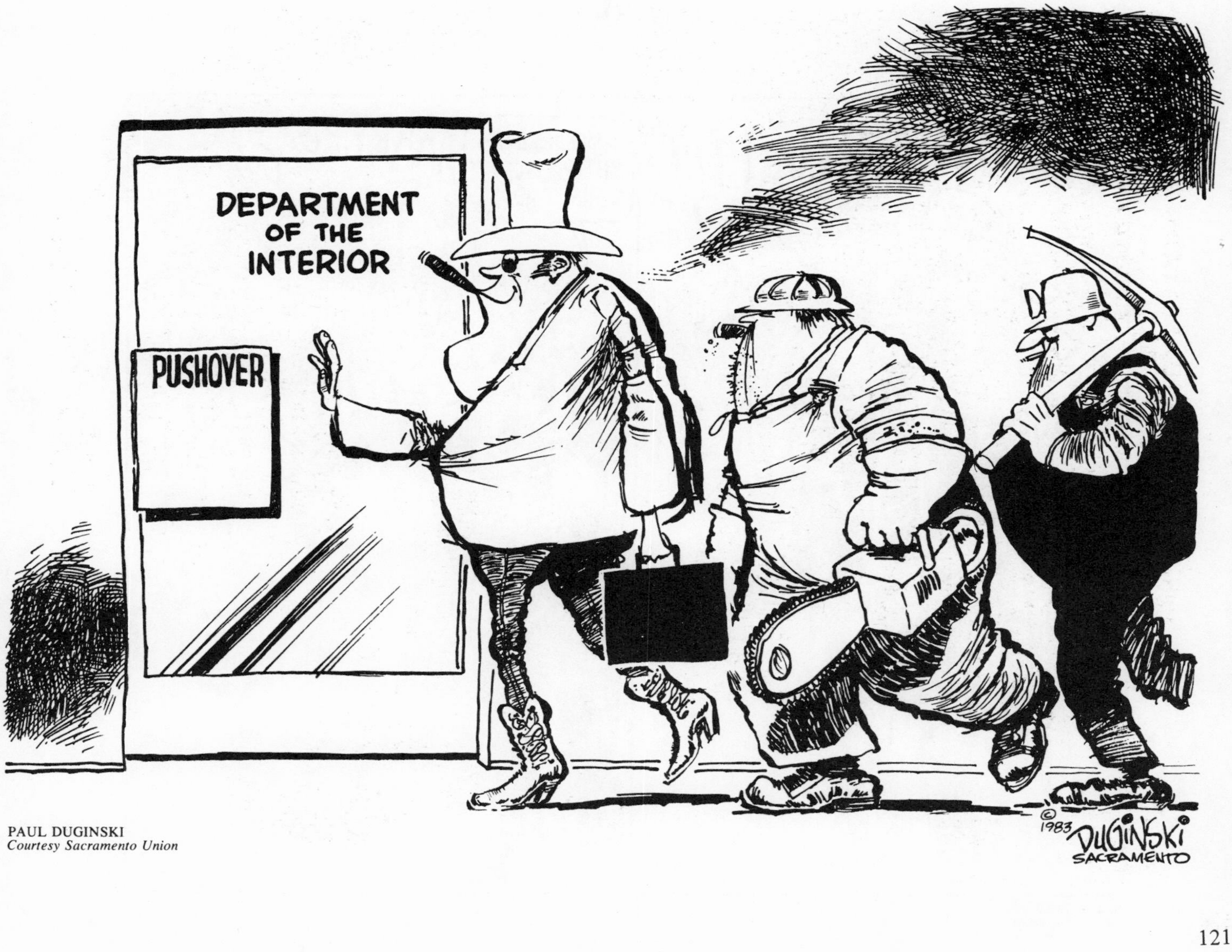
DEPARTMENT
OF THE
INTERIOR
PUSHOVER
© 1983 DUGINSKI SACRAMENTO

PAUL DUGINSKI
Courtesy Sacramento Union

GEORGE DANBY
Courtesy New Haven Register

BILL GARNER
Courtesy Washington Times

LEE JUDGE
Courtesy Kansas City Times

PAUL CONRAD
Courtesy Los Angeles Times

BOB ENGLEHART
Courtesy Hartford Courant

ELDON PLETCHER
Courtesy New Orleans Times–Picayune

BOB TAYLOR
Courtesy Dallas Times–Herald

Environment

Topping the environmental news for 1983 was a scandal that shook the Environmental Protection Agency and caused the top administrator and several staff members to resign or be dismissed. Early in 1983 investigators began delving into the EPA's solid waste division, focusing on its chief, Assistant Administrator Rita M. Lavelle. She was charged with such improprieties as having lunch and dinner meetings with representatives of industries her office was responsible for regulating. She was accused of making "sweetheart" deals that permitted companies to spend less in cleaning up their wastes, or to postpone waste cleanups. Lavelle subsequently was fired as head of the EPA's hazardous waste program, and her boss, EPA Chief Anne Burford, resigned.

According to scientific reports released in June, there exists a direct link between sulfur dioxide emitted from industrial smokestacks and acid rain that has been falling in the northeastern U.S. This acid rain, environmentalists believe, has been responsible for the killing of large numbers of fish, plants, and other forms of aquatic life and the polluting of lakes and streams. The U.S. and Canada signed an agreement in August to study this pollution problem and take whatever preventive measures are deemed necessary.

JIM BORGMAN
Courtesy Cincinnati Enquirer

"I'M MELTING! I'M MELTING! OOOH, MY BEAUTIFUL WASTE DUMPS! MY SHREDDED RECORDS! MY CONTEMPT CHARGES! GONE!... GONE!..."

ROB LAWLOR
Courtesy Philadelphia Daily News

JOHN R. THORNTON
Courtesy Republican Journal

DENNIS RENAULT
Courtesy Sacramento Bee

"Do you want to hear about the splitting headaches or the stabbing back pains?"

Not Much Change In The Scenery

TOM ENGELHARDT
Courtesy St. Louis Post–Dispatch

ED GAMBLE
Courtesy Florida Times–Union

RANDY WICKS
Courtesy Newhall (Calif.) Signal

ED STEIN
Courtesy Rocky Mountain News

IMMY MARGULIES
©Rothco

Old toxic waste containers

New toxic waste containers

ED FISCHER
Courtesy Rochester Post–Bulletin

BRIAN GABLE
Courtesy Regina Leader–Post (Sask.)

FRANK EVERS
Courtesy New York Daily News

CHARLES DANIEL
Courtesy Knoxville Journal

Women's Rights

The proposed Equal Rights Amendment to the U.S. Constitution was re-introduced during the first session of Congress in January. Nothing more was heard on that issue from either house during the year.

The abortion issue cropped up again during the year. On June 15 the U.S. Supreme Court reaffirmed a 1973 decision that women have a constitutional right to an abortion free of virtually any government interference.

The Reagan Administration suffered a degree of embarrassment in August when Barbara Honegger, a low-level political appointee in the Justice Department, resigned with an anti-Reagan blast. She was quoted in a newspaper article as charging that Reagan had failed to keep his promises to the women's movement and that her job of working to eliminate discrimination against women in federal and state laws was a "sham."

Reagan aides continued to express amazement at the president's apparent low standing among women in polls.

JEFF MACNELLY
Courtesy Chicago Tribune

PHIL BISSELL
Courtesy Lowell (Mass.) Sun

...But it's DEAD, my dear!

GARY BROOKINS
Courtesy Richmond Times–Dispatch

SANDY CAMPBELL
Courtesy The Tennessean

ED GAMBLE
Courtesy Florida Times–Union

DANA SUMMERS
Courtesy Orlando Sentinel

H. CLAY BENNETT
Courtesy St. Petersburg Times

Canadian Politics

The Canadian economy rebounded during 1983 from the deep recession that had gripped the country for many months. By June, interest rates had dropped to a six-year low and inflation soon dipped to its lowest level in more than a decade. Car sales and housing starts moved upward, and consumers seemed to have regained confidence in the future.

The overall economic picture, however, was not without flaws. Unemployment remained high, with nearly a million and a half Canadians without a job in June. The total dropped slowly, however, as the year went on.

In spite of the apparent recovery, the popularity of Prime Minister Pierre Trudeau and his Liberal Party continued to decline among the voters. Polls showed that only 27 percent would support the governing Liberal Party if an election were held in July. Trudeau reshuffled his cabinet in an effort to add a new look for an election campaign.

After months of protests by marchers throughout Canada, the government announced in July that U.S. testing of unarmed cruise missiles would be allowed in the northern part of the country. Demonstrators gathered on Parliament Hill in an attempt to persuade the House of Commons to "refuse the cruise." Trudeau stuck to his guns, however, declaring that Canada could not rely on the United States for protection while refusing "to lend a hand when the going gets tough."

BLAINE
Courtesy Hamilton (Ont.) Spectator

EDD ULUSCHAK
Courtesy Edmonton Journal

"Shouldn't they be out gathering winter fuel?"

ADRIAN RAESIDE
Courtesy Times–Colonist (B.C.)

CANADA
GOOSE

CANADA
GOOSED

CRUISE

JAMES F. TODD
Courtesy Cameron Publications

TERRY MOSHER (AISLIN)
Courtesy Montreal Gazette

MIKE GRASTON
Courtesy Windsor Star (Ont.)

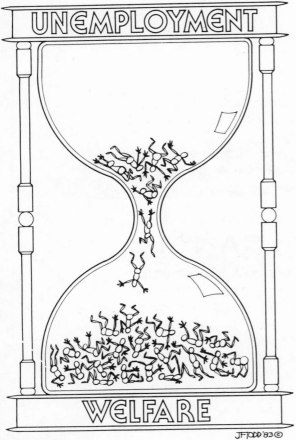

JAMES F. TODD
Courtesy Cameron Publications

JOSH BEUTEL
Courtesy St. John Telegraph–Journal

ADRIAN RAESIDE
Courtesy Times–Colonist (B.C.)

Space

The United States launched some thirty spacecraft during the year, including flights by shuttle crews, a scientific satellite, meteorological satellites, and several communications satellites.

Sally Ride became the first American woman to venture in space in the June flight of the shuttle *Challenger,* and Guion Bluford, Jr., etched his name as the first black in space in the August *Challenger* launch.

The *Columbia* space shuttle was modified so it could be used later as a space laboratory. It was called Spacelab, and was a joint project of the U.S. National Aeronautics and Space Administration and the European Space Agency. It enables scientists to work in space as they do on the ground, moving about freely and consulting with technicians on the ground whenever necessary. Among the projects undertaken were gauging the sun's energy output, an analysis of the upper atmosphere, and the effects of weightlessness on the human body.

President Reagan proposed an all-out effort by space scientists to develop antimissile weapons capable of destroying any weapons aimed at the U.S. The Pentagon already was involved in similar research, but many in Congress made light of the plan, labeling it a "Buck Rogers dream." The Soviets, who also assailed the idea, reportedly already had been testing hunter-killer satellites and other methods of destroying spacecraft or missiles.

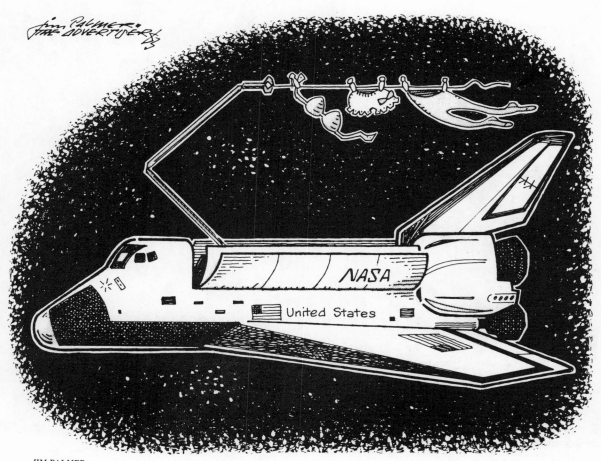

JIM PALMER
Courtesy Montgomery Advertiser

"GOOD GRIEF! BERNICE — YOU'VE NEVER SHOWN AN INTEREST IN THE SPACE SHUTTLE FLIGHTS BEFORE"

JIM MORGAN
Courtesy Spartanburg Herald–Journal

ROB LAWLOR
Courtesy Philadelphia Daily News

Schools

America's public schools were spotlighted in 1983 by a hard-hitting report detailing the steady decline of the public education system. The report declared that "the educational foundations of our society are presently being eroded by a rising tide of mediocrity that threatens our very future as a nation and as a people. What was unimaginable a generation ago has begun to occur—others are matching and surpassing our educational attainments."

The report was prepared by the National Commission on Excellence in Education, an eighteen-member panel appointed by the U.S. secretary of education.

Students in the U.S. do not work as hard or learn as much as those in other industrialized countries, according to the panel's findings. More English, mathematics, and science was recommended, as well as greater emphasis on computer science. The commission also asked state legislatures to consider lengthening the school day to seven hours and the school year to between 200 and 220 days.

MIKE KEEFE
Courtesy Denver Post

BILL SANDERS
Courtesy Milwaukee Journal

JOHN BRANCH
Courtesy San Antonio Express–News

LARRY WRIGHT
Courtesy Detroit News

BILL GRAHAM
Courtesy Arkansas Gazette

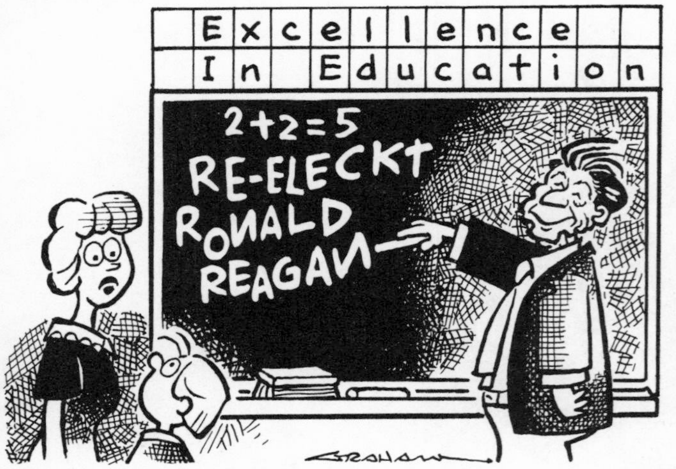

Excellence In Education
2+2=5
RE-ELECKT RONALD REAGAN
GRAHAM

Back to Basics

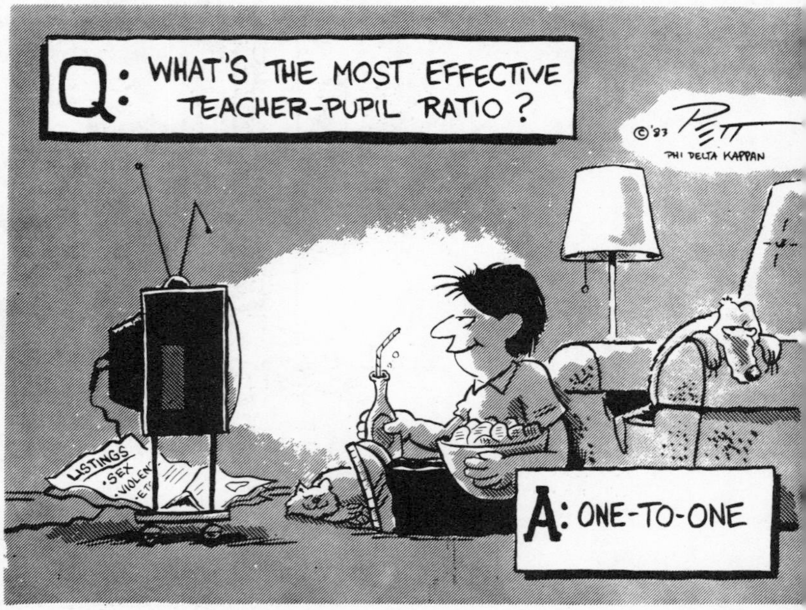

Q: WHAT'S THE MOST EFFECTIVE TEACHER-PUPIL RATIO?
©'83 PETT PHI DELTA KAPPAN
LISTINGS
A: ONE-TO-ONE

JOEL PETT
Courtesy Bloomington Herald–Telephone

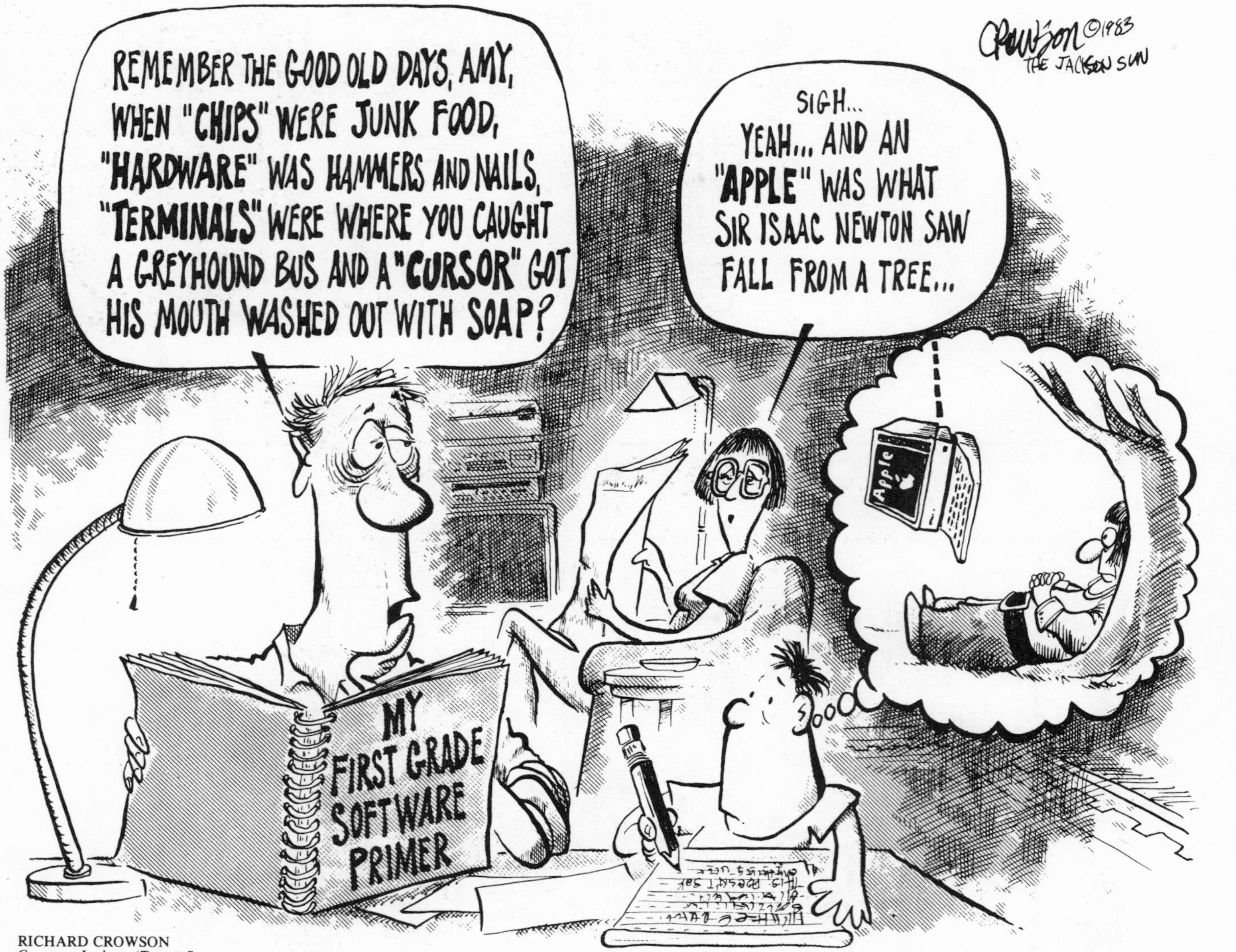

CROWSON ©1983 THE JACKSON SUN
REMEMBER THE GOOD OLD DAYS, AMY, WHEN "CHIPS" WERE JUNK FOOD, "HARDWARE" WAS HAMMERS AND NAILS, "TERMINALS" WERE WHERE YOU CAUGHT A GREYHOUND BUS AND A "CURSOR" GOT HIS MOUTH WASHED OUT WITH SOAP?
SIGH... YEAH... AND AN "APPLE" WAS WHAT SIR ISAAC NEWTON SAW FALL FROM A TREE...
Apple
MY FIRST GRADE SOFTWARE PRIMER

RICHARD CROWSON
Courtesy Jackson (Tenn.) Sun

ART HENRIKSON
©Paddock Publications

STEVE KELLEY
Courtesy San Diego Union

CHARLES BISSELL
Courtesy The Tennessean

"Sure You've Got A Problem But It Won't Help To Throw Money At It!"

145

In Memoriam

In memory of the 269 persons, including Georgia Congressman Larry McDonald, who were murdered by the Soviet Union on September 1, 1983, when Korean Airlines Flight 007 on which they were passengers was ruthlessly shot from the skies in one of history's most barbaric acts.

Many notable personalities died during 1983, including two of the sports world's greatest figures—former heavyweight champion Jack Dempsey and Paul "Bear" Bryant, the winningest college football coach in the history of the game. Bryant amassed a record of 323 victories, topping Amos Alonzo Stagg's old record of 314.

Other well-known figures who died during the year included Mrs. Lillian Carter, mother of former President Jimmy Carter, Turner Catledge, Terence Cardinal Cooke of New York, Buster Crabbe, George Cukor, Dolores del Rio, Roscoe Drummond, Faye Emerson, Marty Feldman, Ira Gershwin, Arthur Godfrey, Freeman Gosden, Senator Henry Jackson, Mary Livingston, Raymond Massey, David Niven, Pat O'Brien, Frank Reynolds, Marty Robbins, Artur Rubenstein, Jessica Savitch, Norma Shearer, Walter Slezak, Gloria Swanson, Jack Webb, and Tennessee Williams.

YOU ARE NOW ENTERING SOVIET AIR SPACE

CAMPBELL
SANDY CAMPBELL
Courtesy The Tennessean

VERN THOMPSON
Courtesy Lawton (Okla.) Constitution

ED ASHLEY
Courtesy Toledo Blade

. . . and Other Issues

Computers remained a big issue throughout the year. Consumers looking for personal computers found a wide variety of models available at ever-declining prices, and competition within the industry began to weed out the weaker sisters. Texas Instruments, after losses of $229 million in the first two quarters, announced it was pulling out of the home computer field.

A group of computer raiders in Milwaukee stunned some experts when they tapped sophisticated government computers at the nuclear weapons laboratory at Los Alamos, New Mexico, and other systems at the Sloan-Kettering Cancer Center in New York. Obviously, there was a clear and immediate need for improved security for major computer systems.

The West German magazine *Der Stern* proudly announced in April that it had purchased sixty-two volumes of the diaries and other writings of Adolf Hitler. Reportedly, $4 million was paid for the works, and the London *Sunday Times* contracted for publication rights. Many experts immediately doubted the works' authenticity—and they were right. It was indeed a fraud, and arrests were made.

ED GAMBLE
Courtesy Florida Times–Union

TOM ADDISON
Courtesy Greenville Piedmont

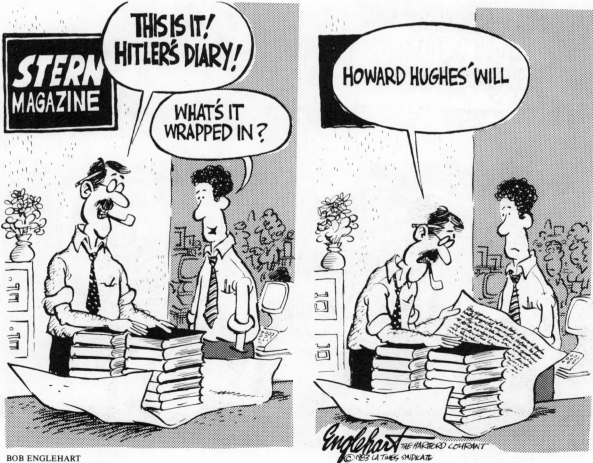

BOB ENGLEHART
Courtesy Hartford Courant

CHAN LOWE
Courtesy Oklahoma City Times

JANE BYRNE JACK HIGGINS
Courtesy Chicago Sun-Times

JOEL PETT
*Courtesy Bloomington
Herald–Telephone*

DOUGLAS REGALIA
Courtesy Contra Costa Sun

ANGEL ZAMARRIPA
Mexico

TOM DARCY
Courtesy Newsday

TERRY MOSHER (AISLIN)
Courtesy Montreal Gazette

JIM ORTON
Courtesy Computerworld

'JENNY, WHY DOESN'T SOMEBODY STOP US BEFORE WE REALLY MESS THINGS UP?'

BRIAN GABLE
Courtesy Regina Leader-Post (Sask.)

MATT MAYER
Courtesy Massillon Evening Independent

PAUL DUGINSKI
Courtesy Sacramento Union

153

DANI AGUILA
Courtesy Filipino Reporter

ETTA HULME
Courtesy Ft. Worth Star–Telegram

DAN WASSERMAN
© Los Angeles Times Syndicate

RICKY NOBILE
Courtesy Bolivar (Miss.) Commercial

JIM DOBBINS
Courtesy Union–Leader

155

Future News Item: IN THE WAKE OF THE SECRETARY OF AGRICULTURE'S FEEDING HIS FAMILY FOR ONE WEEK ON FOOD STAMPS, DEFENSE SECRETARY WEINBERGER TRIES TO RUN HIS CAR FOR A WEEK USING ONLY SIX MILLION DOLLARS WORTH OF MILITARY SPARE PARTS.

JOHN STAMPONE

Past Award Winners

PULITZER PRIZE EDITORIAL CARTOON

1922—Rollin Kirby, New York World
1924—J. N. Darling, New York Herald Tribune
1925—Rollin Kirby, New York World
1926—D. R. Fitzpatrick, St. Louis Post-Dispatch
1927—Nelson Harding, Brooklyn Eagle
1928—Nelson Harding, Brooklyn Eagle
1928—Nelson Harding, Brooklyn Eagle
1929—Rollin Kirby, New York World
1930—Charles Macauley, Brooklyn Eagle
1931—Edmund Duffy, Baltimore Sun
1932—John T. McCutcheon, Chicago Tribune
1933—H. M. Talburt, Washington Daily News
1934—Edmund Duffy, Baltimore Sun
1935—Ross A. Lewis, Milwaukee Journal
1937—C. D. Batchelor, New York Daily News
1938—Vaughn Shoemaker, Chicago Daily News
1939—Charles G. Werner, Daily Oklahoman
1940—Edmund Duffy, Baltimore Sun
1941—Jacob Burck, Chicago Times
1942—Herbert L. Block, Newspaper Enterprise Association
1943—Jay N. Darling, New York Herald Tribune
1944—Clifford K. Berryman, Washington Star
1945—Bill Mauldin, United Feature Syndicate
1946—Bruce Russell, Los Angeles Times
1947—Vaughn Shoemaker, Chicago Daily News
1948—Reuben L. (Rube) Goldberg, New York Sun
1949—Lute Pease, Newark Evening News
1950—James T. Berryman, Washington Star
1951—Reginald W. Manning, Arizona Republic
1952—Fred L. Packer, New York Mirror
1953—Edward D. Kuekes, Cleveland Plain Dealer
1954—Herbert L. Block, Washington Post
1955—Daniel R. Fitzpatrick, St. Louis Post-Dispatch
1956—Robert York, Louisville Times
1957—Tom Little, Nashville Tennessean
1958—Bruce M. Shanks, Buffalo Evening News
1959—Bill Mauldin, St. Louis Post-Dispatch
1961—Carey Orr, Chicago Tribune
1962—Edmund S. Valtman, Hartford Times
1963—Frank Miller, Des Moines Register
1964—Paul Conrad, Denver Post
1966—Don Wright, Miami News
1967—Patrick B. Oliphant, Denver Post
1968—Eugene Gray Payne, Charlotte Observer
1969—John Fischetti, Chicago Daily News
1970—Thomas F. Darcy, Newsday
1971—Paul Conrad, Los Angeles Times
1972—Jeffrey K. MacNelly, Richmond News Leader
1974—Paul Szep, Boston Globe
1975—Garry Trudeau, Universal Press Syndicate
1976—Tony Auth, Philadelphia Enquirer
1977—Paul Szep, Boston Globe

1978—Jeff MacNelly, Richmond News Leader
1979—Herbert Block, Washington Post
1980—Don Wright, Miami News
1981—Herbert Block, Washington Post
1982—Ben Sargent, Austin American-Statesman
1983—Dick Locher, Chicago Tribune

NOTE: Pulitzer Prize Award was not given 1923, 1936, 1960, 1965, and 1973.

SIGMA DELTA CHI EDITORIAL CARTOON

1942—Jacob Burck, Chicago Times
1943—Charles Werner, Chicago Sun
1944—Henry Barrow, Associated Press
1945—Reuben L. Goldberg, New York Sun
1946—Dorman H. Smith, Newspaper Enterprise Association
1947—Bruce Russell, Los Angeles Times
1948—Herbert Block, Washington Post
1949—Herbert Block, Washington Post
1950—Bruce Russell, Los Angeles Times
1951—Herbert Block, Washington Post, and
        Bruce Russell, Los Angeles Times
1952—Cecil Jensen, Chicago Daily News
1953—John Fischetti, Newspaper Enterprise Association
1954—Calvin Alley, Memphis Commercial Appeal
1955—John Fischetti, Newspaper Enterprise Association
1956—Herbert Block, Washington Post
1957—Scott Long, Minneapolis Tribune
1958—Clifford H. Baldowski, Atlanta Constitution
1959—Charles G. Brooks, Birmingham News
1960—Dan Dowling, New York Herald-Tribune
1961—Frank Interlandi, Des Moines Register
1962—Paul Conrad, Denver Post
1963—William Mauldin, Chicago Sun-Times
1964—Charles Bissell, Nashville Tennessean
1965—Roy Justus, Minneapolis Star
1966—Patrick Oliphant, Denver Post
1967—Eugene Payne, Charlotte Observer
1968—Paul Conrad, Los Angeles Times
1969—William Mauldin, Chicago Sun-Times
1970—Paul Conrad, Los Angeles Times
1971—Hugh Haynie, Louisville Courier-Journal
1972—William Mauldin, Chicago Sun-Times
1973—Paul Szep, Boston Globe
1974—Mike Peters, Dayton Daily News
1975—Tony Auth, Philadelphia Enquirer
1976—Paul Szep, Boston Globe
1977—Don Wright, Miami News
1978—Jim Borgman, Cincinnati Enquirer
1979—John P. Trever, Albuquerque Journal
1980—Paul Conrad, Los Angeles Times
1981—Paul Conrad, Los Angeles Times
1982—Dick Locher, Chicago Tribune

NATIONAL HEADLINERS CLUB AWARD EDITORIAL CARTOON

1938—C. D. Batchelor, New York Daily News
1939—John Knott, Dallas News
1940—Herbert Block, Newspaper Enterprise Association
1941—Charles H. Sykes, Philadelphia Evening Ledger
1942—Jerry Doyle, Philadelphia Record
1943—Vaughn Shoemaker, Chicago Daily News
1944—Roy Justus, Sioux City Journal
1945—F. O. Alexander, Philadelphia Bulletin
1946—Hank Barrow, Associated Press
1947—Cy Hungerford, Pittsburgh Post-Gazette
1948—Tom Little, Nashville Tennessean
1949—Bruce Russell, Los Angeles Times
1950—Dorman Smith, Newspaper Enterprise Association
1951—C. G. Werner, Indianapolis Star
1952—John Fischetti, Newspaper Enterprise Association
1953—James T. Berryman and Gib Crockett, Washington Star
1954—Scott Long, Minneapolis Tribune
1955—Leo Thiele, Los Angeles Mirror-News
1956—John Milt Morris, Associated Press
1957—Frank Miller, Des Moines Register
1958—Burris Jenkins, Jr., New York Journal-American
1959—Karl Hubenthal, Los Angeles Examiner
1960—Don Hesse, St. Louis Globe-Democrat
1961—L. D. Warren, Cincinnati Enquirer
1962—Franklin Morse, Los Angeles Mirror
1963—Charles Bissell, Nashville Tennessean
1964—Lou Grant, Oakland Tribune
1965—Merle R. Tingley, London (Ont.) Free Press
1966—Hugh Haynie, Louisville Courier-Journal
1967—Jim Berry, Newspaper Enterprise Association
1968—Warren King, New York News
1969—Larry Barton, Toledo Blade
1970—Bill Crawford, Newspaper Enterprise Association
1971—Ray Osrin, Cleveland Plain Dealer
1972—Jacob Burck, Chicago Sun-Times
1973—Ranan Lurie, New York Times
1974—Tom Darcy, Newsday
1975—Bill Sanders, Milwaukee Journal
1976—No award given
1977—Paul Szep, Boston Globe
1978—Dwane Powell, Raleigh News and Observer
1979—Pat Oliphant, Washington Star
1980—Don Wright, Miami News
1981—Bill Garner, Memphis Commercial Appeal
1982—Mike Peters, Dayton Daily News
1983—Doug Marlette, Charlotte Observer

NATIONAL NEWSPAPER AWARD/CANADA EDITORIAL CARTOON

1949—Jack Boothe, Toronto Globe and Mail
1950—James G. Reidford, Montreal Star
1951—Len Norris, Vancouver Sun
1952—Robert La Palme, Le Devoir, Montreal
1953—Robert W. Chambers, Halifax Chronicle-Herald
1954—John Collins, Montreal Gazette
1955—Merle R. Tingley, London Free Press
1956—James G. Reidford, Toronto Globe and Mail
1957—James G. Reidford, Toronto Globe and Mail
1958—Raoul Hunter, Le Soleil, Quebec
1959—Duncan Macpherson, Toronto Star
1960—Duncan Macpherson, Toronto Star
1961—Ed McNally, Montreal Star
1962—Duncan Macpherson, Toronto Star
1963—Jan Kamienski, Winnipeg Tribune
1964—Ed McNally, Montreal Star
1965—Duncan Macpherson, Toronto Star
1966—Robert W. Chambers, Halifax Chronicle-Herald
1967—Raoul Hunter, Le Soleil, Quebec
1968—Roy Peterson, Vancouver Sun
1969—Edward Uluschak, Edmonton Journal
1970—Duncan Macpherson, Toronto Daily Star
1971—Yardley Jones, Toronto Sun
1972—Duncan Macpherson, Toronto Star
1973—John Collins, Montreal Gazette
1974—Blaine, Hamilton Spectator
1975—Roy Peterson, Vancouver Sun
1976—Andy Donato, Toronto Sun
1977—Terry Mosher, Montreal Gazette
1978—Terry Mosher, Montreal Gazette
1979—Edd Uluschak, Edmonton Journal
1980—Vic Roschkov, Toronto Star
1981—Tom Innes, Calgary Herald
1982—Blaine, Hamilton Spectator

OVERSEAS PRESS CLUB AWARD EDITORIAL CARTOON

1971—Tom Darcy, Newsday
1972—Don Wright, Miami News
1973—Tom Darcy, Newsday
1974—Warren King, New York Daily News
1975—Tony Auth, Philadelphia Inquirer
1976—Tony Auth, Philadelphia Inquirer
1977—Warren King, New York Daily News
1978—Ed Fischer, Omaha World-Herald
1979—Jim Morin, Miami Herald
1980—Don Wright, Miami News
1981—Paul Conrad, Los Angeles Times
1982—Don Wright, Miami News
1983—Dick Locher, Chicago Tribune

Index

INDEX